# Intentional Learning:
# A Process for
# Learning to Learn
# in the
# Accounting Curriculum

Marlene C. Francis
Timothy C. Mulder
Joan S. Stark

American Accounting Association
5717 Bessie Drive
Sarasota, Florida 34233

# EXECUTIVE SUMMARY

In its first position paper, the Accounting Education Change Commission stressed the importance of lifelong learning for professional accountants. The Commission urged that accounting educators include learning to learn in the accounting curriculum. This monograph discusses learning to learn in terms of the process and attributes of intentional learning. It is intended to help accounting faculty incorporate learning processes into their accounting courses.

We define learning to learn as a process of acquiring, understanding, and using a variety of strategies to improve one's ability to attain and apply knowledge, a process which results from, leads to, and enhances a questioning spirit and a lifelong desire to learn. We describe the process as intentional learning, that is, learning with self-directed purpose, intending and choosing to learn and how and what to learn. Intentional learning involves five attributes of learning: questioning, organizing, connecting, reflecting, and adapting.

To help students learn to learn, faculty need to know some of the characteristics that influence student learning. Understanding student intellectual development can help faculty plan courses that lead students to mature intellectually. Knowledge of learning styles, their own and their students', can help faculty develop assignments that include a variety of learning experiences. A review of motivation theory and conscious consideration of course goals can help faculty plan courses that challenge and involve students in effective intentional learning.

Teaching and the role of the teacher influence the development of intentional learning. Faculty can create academic plans and develop teaching strategies that help students develop the attributes of intentional learning. The teacher's role becomes mentoring and coaching while the learner's role becomes questioning, organizing, connecting, and reflecting on knowledge and adapting it to use. We suggest how such common teaching/learning experiences as lectures, reading, discussions, group learning, problems and cases, writing and technology can be adapted to enhance intentional learning in the accounting curriculum. The teaching context and evaluation procedures can also be adapted to focus on learning and using the attributes of intentional learning. Examples of innovations at the program, course, and assignment levels are included to suggest how accounting faculty may begin to integrate learning to learn into their own teaching.

# CONTENTS

**FIGURES**

# FOREWORD

The mission of the Accounting Education Change Commission is to improve the academic preparation of accountants, so that entrants to the profession will possess the skills, knowledge, and values and attitudes required for success in accounting career paths. This mission is consistent with the objectives of the American Accounting Association's "Bedford Committee" report and the Sponsoring Firms' white paper, *"Perspectives on Education: Capabilities for Success in the Accounting Profession."*

The Commission has undertaken a number of initiatives to carry out its charge, including the publication of a number of position and issue statements. Position Statement No. 1 of the Commission describes the objectives of accounting education, and states that "The overriding objective of accounting programs should be to teach students to learn on their own." Appendix A to Position Statement No. 1 describes learning to learn. However, the Commission felt that a more thorough analysis of the process of learning to learn, along with guidance on how to incorporate experiences into accounting curricula that would promote learning to learn, was needed. This monograph was commissioned in response to that need.

The authors bring a variety of perspectives and experience to the topic of learning to learn. Dr. Marlene Francis is currently a visiting scholar at the University of Michigan, working on projects related to college curriculum and history and both liberal and professional education. She is a trustee of Kalamazoo College and has taught or been an administrator at the University of Akron, the University of Michigan, and Cleary College. Timothy Mulder is associate professor of accounting at Davenport College, a practicing CPA, and a Ph.D. candidate in the Center for the Study of Higher and Postsecondary Education at the University of Michigan. His dissertation research explores the liberal education competencies used by professional accountants. Dr. Joan Stark is professor of higher education at the University of Michigan and editor of the *Review of Higher Education.* She served on the Accounting Education Change Commission from 1989 to 1994, has held faculty and administrative positions at the University of Michigan, Syracuse University, and Goucher College, and has published widely on college course planning, curriculum development, and professional education. The Commission is very grateful to the authors for their efforts in preparing this monograph.

Richard E. Flaherty
Executive Director
Accounting Education Change Commission
Tempe, Arizona
April 1995

Jan R. Williams
Director of Education
American Accounting Association
Sarasota, Florida
April 1995

# PREFACE

For over a decade, accounting educators and practitioners have been working together to change the way accountants are educated. Changes in the field have prompted practitioners to reconsider the qualifications accountants will need for success in the future. Employers of accounting graduates are calling for a wide range of intellectual and interpersonal skills, as well as basic knowledge of business and accounting. They are calling especially for accounting graduates who are prepared to be lifelong learners in their practice of accounting.

Accounting educators are responding to the concerns of practitioners by exploring new approaches to curriculum, new courses and assignments, and new ways to teach accounting. Accounting education is shifting from a focus on memorizing rules and working problems to an increased emphasis on student learning. This monograph is part of this emphasis. We suggest introducing into accounting education a process of intentional learning, that is, learning with a plan, intent, intensity, and self determination while learning the practice of accounting.

## 0.1 Background

In 1986, the American Accounting Association's Committee on the Future Structure, Content, and Scope of Accounting Education presented an important report to the accounting education community. This report, "Future Accounting Education: Preparing for the Expanding Profession" (generally referred to by the chairman's name as the Bedford Report), called for major changes in how future accountants were to be educated. The report made 28 specific recommendations, all aimed at achieving two main goals: "(1) approach accounting education as an information development and distribution function for economic decision making, and (2) emphasize students' learning to learn as the primary classroom objective."

The Bedford Report was followed in 1989 by a major position statement by the then "Big Eight" public accounting firms, "Perspectives on Education: Capabilities for Success in the Accounting Profession." The "Perspectives" statement focused on the qualifications needed by future accountants and challenged accounting educators to change the accounting curriculum to emphasize these new capabilities. In particular, the statement urged educators to move to an approach that would integrate the capabilities required for success into the whole accounting curriculum. The firms that sponsored the report committed $5 million over seven years to support curriculum improvement. Specifically, these funds supported creation of the Accounting Education Change Commission (AECC) and the Commission's funding of a dozen grants to colleges and universities for significant curriculum change projects.

The projects underwritten by the AECC involved a variety of approaches to curriculum change in four-year and two-year undergraduate programs, and at the graduate level. The Commission maintains that many different approaches to accounting education can produce the desired results; each program should find the way that works best for its institution and students. The AECC does, however, advocate a set of common objectives for accounting education. It has published a series of position papers and issues statements intended to stimulate discussion and shape curriculum change.

In its first formal position paper, "Objectives of Education for Accountants," the AECC maintained that because the profession is changing rapidly, it is no longer possible to prepare graduates fully to be accountants when they enter the profession. Instead, the formal educational program must prepare graduates to become professional accountants through a lifetime of experience, growth, and learning.

In an appendix to this first position paper (included here as Appendix A), the AECC stressed the need for accounting graduates to become lifelong learners. The Commission believes that accounting education must change from its predominant focus on the acquisition of knowledge to a new emphasis on learning to learn. In the position paper, the Commission defined learning to learn as "developing skills and strategies that help one [to] learn more effectively and to use these effective learning strategies to learn through his or her lifetime." The Commission believes that future accountants should be able to apply learning strategies to their undergraduate studies and also adapt them to continuing education experiences throughout their careers.

The AECC appendix on learning to learn includes three issues that accounting programs should address: content, process, and attitudes. While recognizing that all three issues are important, we have focused discussion in this monograph on process. To learn effectively and to remain a learner throughout life, a person needs conscious understanding of the learning process. This understanding is at the heart of our approach to learning to learn. It involves developing skills and strategies for learning from a variety of sources and in different settings. We address content (what is learned) primarily through examples, and we discuss the attitude of inquiry as motivation for learning. We believe that by focusing on process, particularly on several key attributes of learning, this monograph will help accounting faculty introduce elements of learning to learn into the accounting curriculum.

## 0.2 Independent Learners and Intentional Learning

Most accounting faculty are more comfortable teaching accounting content than teaching the processes and attitudes required for lifelong learning. That is why we have chosen to focus on process here. This monograph is intended to assist faculty by developing the concept of intentional learning and suggesting specific attributes that can be practiced by students in accounting classes. Ultimately, of course, students must do their own learning and develop their own individual skills. Our concept of intentional learning is intended to help them do this.

Descriptions of future accounting professionals emphasize that they must become "independent learners." This term suggests a sense of freedom, of learning on one's own that certainly fits the needs of the profession. It implies a broad set of competencies: the ability to be good, analytical readers of complex, technical materials; skill at seeking out information and researching answers to business problems; ability to distinguish between useful and irrelevant material. Future accounting professionals need to use these skills to learn quickly, under pressure, and on their own, to handle the challenges of their profession. Yet these skills are learned, not automatically acquired. By consciously practicing a learning process, accounting students can prepare themselves to become independent learners as professionals.

Learning to learn is perceived as an essential skill for independent learners. However, the concept of learning to learn is at present broad and not clearly defined. In attempting to describe learning to learn for accounting professors, we sought to develop a set of terms and processes that could be immediately adapted for use in a variety of settings. We focus on a process and a set of attributes that we believe to be basic to development of the ability to learn to learn. We believe that the process can be purposely used to develop the skills of independent learning.

We deliberately chose the term "intentional learning" to emphasize the importance of intent, purpose, and intensity in the learning process. Both denotatively and connotatively, the term "intentional learning" suggests the planned, conscious commitment to continuing learning expected of accounting professionals. In this monograph, we propose five attributes of intentional learning—questioning, organizing, connecting, reflecting, adapting—and discuss them as essential activities for learning to learn. We suggest that practicing the attributes of intentional learning will involve students in learning to learn and ultimately will produce independent learners.

The process of intentional learning is introduced here as a way to help accounting students become independent learners. It is seen as a process that can be readily introduced into accounting courses and curricula regardless of the type or level of content being taught. Our description of intentional learning is an attempt to simplify and operationalize what psychologists call "metacognition" and accounting educators seem to mean by "learning to learn." We do not claim that intentional learning includes all that accounting professionals need to know or be able to do. We do maintain, however, that introducing the attributes of intentional learning can be an effective way to help accounting students learn to learn and begin to become independent learners.

## 0.3 Audience

This monograph is intended for accounting faculty who are interested in introducing some elements of learning to learn into their courses. It should be helpful in planning changes at both the course and program levels. Accounting faculty, like their students, must continue to be learners. They should find the monograph helpful in promoting their own professional growth as well as in their work as faculty. The monograph may thus be useful in faculty development efforts, as well as in promoting curricular change.

We assume that most readers of the monograph will be faculty in four- or five-year accounting programs. They are actively engaged in teaching and they are interested in considering the AECC recommendations for accounting education. Their students are preparing to be professional accountants working in public accounting or in businesses, government, and non-profit corporations. However, we recognize that many accounting students begin their professional education at two-year colleges and that many of the issues discussed here apply in most postsecondary education settings. Thus, while our discussion and examples focus on four- and five-year accounting programs, we believe that the material presented here will be useful in a variety of educational institutions.

Because our readers are primarily interested in accounting education, not in educational psychology, we have consciously avoided the most esoteric language of specialists in learning. Instead, we have sought to interpret current understandings of the learning process in general terms and to provide some accounting examples and applications. By including real-life stories and experiences, we have tried to make the monograph enjoyable as well as informative for our readers.

## 0.4 The Monograph

The AECC commissioned this monograph as a brief introduction to the basic concepts of learning to learn. The focus here is on theory and principle and on applications to accounting education, not on research questions and results. We have made no attempt to break new ground nor to present original research. We have, instead, attempted to distill what is known into a clear and practical presentation of key ideas about learning to learn. The process we describe is generic to any field, but we have tried to make it especially useful by introducing examples from accounting. Our goal is to offer a brief guide that will help shape change in the accounting curriculum.

The concept of learning to learn has been developed over the past two or three decades. The phrase itself derives from a number of research orientations and may have a variety of technical definitions, as well as common, every day definitions used by laymen. While accounting educators do not need detailed knowledge of this background, they do need information about the concepts behind and the educational changes implicit within the phrase. Most of all, they need information about how to apply learning to learn concepts to their own teaching and curricula.

This monograph attempts to meet these needs. It begins with a description of accountants as learners and professionals, and presents a definition of and perspectives on learning to learn. The second chapter introduces a new concept—the intentional learning process—and the attributes of intentional learning as a manageable approach to teaching students to be independent learners. The third chapter presents characteristics of learners which influence their attitudes toward learning and their ability to learn. The fourth chapter discusses the learning process and teaching strategies that can encourage students to learn. Finally, the concluding chapter addresses the implementation of learning to learn in the accounting curriculum, problems to consider in implementing change, and some suggestions for using intentional learning in accounting practice.

The monograph does not pretend to offer all the answers for all the faculty who may be reading it. There is no guarantee that any specific idea presented here will work in any particular situation. There are, however, a variety of ideas and strategies suggested and a number of resources mentioned. We believe that most accounting faculty will find here a number of ideas that they can immediately adapt for use in their own programs and with their own courses and students.

In an attempt to make this monograph as readable as possible, we have adopted several conventions. First, we have chosen to minimize citations as much as possible. Our purpose has been to interpret and make useful and readable the work of scholars in several fields. We acknowledge here our gratitude to multiple sources which we have used freely. Responsibility for any errors in interpretation is ours.

In order to avoid the awkwardness of such phrases as he/she, we have chosen to alternate pronoun references by chapter, using either <u>he</u> or <u>she</u> when gender references cannot be avoided. Thus, pronoun references to students in Chapters 1, 3, and 5 are <u>she</u>, and references in Chapters 2 and 4 are <u>he</u>. Faculty references are opposite to students, that is, faculty in Chapters 1, 3, and 5 are <u>he</u>, in chapters 2 and 4 <u>she</u>.

To assist readers who wish to pursue our topic further, we have included a list of references and resources. The list includes references to all the primary sources used in the monograph and some resources that we believe will be helpful. The list could, of course, have been much longer, but we tried to be selective and suggest readings that would be particularly useful for accounting faculty.

Faculty readers of early drafts of our work have consistently asked for specific examples. We have tried to provide these both in the text and in "example boxes" scattered through each chapter. These "boxes" are intended to introduce very specific examples, illustrations, or advice related to the material under discussion. In addition, we have provided a number of figures that are intended to demonstrate and clarify the ideas being presented. In these ways we have tried to address the needs of accounting faculty for brief, informative, readable material on introducing learning to learn in the accounting curriculum.

## 0.5 Acknowledgments

In undertaking this monograph, we relied extensively on the work of scholars in several related fields. Their work is acknowledged in the references listed at the end of the book. Members of the sponsoring Accounting Education Change Commission were helpful in developing and supporting the monograph. We are particularly grateful to Doyle Z. Williams, former chairman and executive director of the AECC; Richard E. Flaherty, current executive director; James Loebbecke, chair of the monograph review committee; Mel O'Connor, our liaison with the AECC; and Jan Williams, Director of Education of the American Accounting Association and AECC member. We also appreciate the helpful editorial suggestions of AECC member Katherine Schipper, and ideas and encouragement offered by Professors Doris de Lespinasse, Adrian College; Thomas Frecka, Notre Dame; and Rob Ingram and colleagues at the University of Alabama. Linda Stiles, who prepared the manuscript, was again an invaluable and much appreciated assistant and colleague.

# Chapter One
# ACCOUNTANTS AS LEARNERS

In an article addressed to practicing accountants, Robert Smith, professor of adult education at Northern Illinois University, asks, "Have you learned how to learn? Or have you learned how to be taught?" The distinction he draws is important for accounting faculty and their students. It suggests the difference between the kind of passive learning that has been said to characterize much accounting education in the past, and the more active, independent learning that is being envisioned by the AECC for accountants in the future.

The student who has learned how to be taught is passive and diligent. She is comfortable in the lecture room, taking notes and "receiving knowledge" from the instructor. This student probably has some effective study habits, knows how to read and remember what the textbook and authorities have to say, and has developed successful techniques for memorizing vocabulary, facts, the rules of the field. She is good at accumulating knowledge. This student is very likely to do well in most college courses in the United States today.

On the other hand, the student who has learned to learn approaches new knowledge differently. This student asks questions about new material, connects it with what she already knows, organizes facts and rules into concepts and principles. Even more important, this student is aware of a variety of learning strategies, knows how to use them, and consciously chooses the strategies that will be most effective for a specific learning task. Most important of all, this student enjoys learning, wants to learn more, and will continue to learn out of personal and professional interest. This is the student accounting educators hope to attract to the new accounting curriculum. This is the student who will be prepared to meet the challenges of the profession in the future.

## 1.1 Accounting Professionals for the Future

Future accountants will need to be as proficient in communication skills as they are with numbers, as comfortable in a committee as they are with a calculator, as ready to learn and apply a new theory as they are to interpret an old rule. The Bedford Report, the "Perspectives" paper, and the AECC all stress that future accounting professionals will need to learn more than the technical accounting knowledge usually emphasized in accounting education. We review here some lists of expanded competencies that will be required and suggest their relationship to the focus on learning to learn in the new accounting curriculum.

In its first position paper, the AECC included a composite profile of the capabilities needed by accounting graduates. These included the following eight categories (see Appendix B for the detailed profile).

1. General Knowledge
2. Intellectual Skills
3. Interpersonal Skills
4. Communication Skills
5. Organizational and Business Knowledge
6. Accounting Knowledge
7. Accounting Skills
8. Personal Capacities and Attitudes

Learning to learn is implied but not specifically listed in the profile. Creative thinking, energy, motivation, and a commitment to lifelong learning are among the nine characteristics listed under Personal Capacities and Attitudes. The list of Intellectual Skills includes other characteristics that contribute to a graduate's ability to continue learning. The composite profile includes a wide range of knowledge, interests, skills, and characteristics that both include and require continuing involvement in learning.

A similar list of capabilities needed for the practice of accountancy was compiled by accounting faculty at Brigham Young University (BYU). As part of their curriculum reform effort, BYU faculty identified a set of 27 expanded competencies needed by future accounting professionals. These competencies are listed in abbreviated form in Figure 1.1 (Deppe et al., 1991).

Of the 27 competencies, only four are related to direct knowledge of accounting and only three more are related to a study of the business environment. Lifelong learning is presented here as a professional competency, but the ability to continue learning is also inherent in several of the other competencies. Many of the competencies could be gained in general education or accounting experience, but if accounting students are to take them seriously and develop them adequately, these competencies need also to be included in the accounting curriculum.

BYU faculty surveyed practicing accountants to learn if, where, and in what degree they had developed each competency: precollege, undergraduate program, graduate program, after college employment or not developed. The respondents were all accounting professionals who had graduated within the past five years. Both masters and bachelors graduates indicated that the majority of the competencies had been developed during employment. Only competency 13, Understanding the Fundamentals of Accounting, Auditing, and Tax, was indicated by both groups as primarily developed during college. On ethical values and motivation for lifelong learning, about one-third of both groups indicated that the competency had been developed during precollege years. The study sample included graduates of 158 colleges and universities and the results suggest that the expanded competencies needed by the accounting profession are not being taught in many accounting programs.

These findings underscore the need to reform accounting education. They also suggest the responsibility of the profession itself to encourage and facilitate continuing growth of its practitioners. If future accounting professionals are to develop the expanded competencies required by the field, current practitioners and professors must work together to reform both accounting education and the early employment experience. As urged by the Bedford Report, the "Perspectives" paper, and the AECC, an emphasis on learning to learn in the new accounting curriculum can begin the

**FIGURE 1.1**

EXPANDED COMPETENCIES
FOR THE PRACTICE OF ACCOUNTANCY

COMMUNICATION SKILLS
 1. Writing
 2. Oral presentation
 3. Reading and critiquing written work
 4. Listening
 5. Understanding interpersonal dynamics
INFORMATION DEVELOPMENT AND DISTRIBUTION SKILLS
 6. Understanding the role of information technology in business
 7. Ability to plan, implement, and evaluate an information system
 8. Applying programming skills to business problems
DECISION MAKING SKILLS
 9. Solve unstructured problems in unfamiliar settings
10. Induce general conclusions from specific situations
11. Set priorities within limited resources
KNOWLEDGE OF ACCOUNTING, AUDITING, AND TAX
12. Knowing the purpose and elements of financial statements
13. Understanding the fundamentals of accounting, auditing, and tax
14. Knowing how to gather, summarize, and analyze financial data
15. Applying the decision rules of the accounting model
KNOWLEDGE OF BUSINESS AND THE ENVIRONMENT
16. Understanding economic, social, and cultural forces
17. Knowing how businesses work and are managed
18. Knowing how financial markets and funding institutions work
PROFESSIONALISM
19. Identifying ethical issues and applying personal values to them
20. Motivation to continue lifelong learning
21. Dealing effectively with imposed pressures
LEADERSHIP DEVELOPMENT
22. Working effectively with diverse groups of people
23. Organizing and delegating tasks
24. Motivating others
25. Resolving conflict
26. Understanding methods of organizational change
27. Using data, exercising judgment, evaluating risks, and solving real-world
    problems

process of expanding competencies and preparing future accountants to continue developing their professional abilities.

While a member of the AECC, Stark reviewed proposals for funding accounting curriculum change projects. While each proposal was different, they shared a number of potential outcomes. Stark prepared the list of desired student outcomes in Figure 1.2 based on an analysis of grant proposals funded by the AECC.

---

**FIGURE 1.2**

**DESIRED STUDENT OUTCOMES
OF REVISED ACCOUNTING CURRICULA**
(based on an analysis of funded grant proposals)

A. Working with people to achieve tasks
    1. Interpersonal skills
    2. Teamwork
    3. Leadership skills
    4. Understanding the work environment
    5. Communication skills

B. Solving problems (general)
    1. Critical and analytical thinking skills
    2. Solving unstructured (as well as structured) problems
    3. Making decisions

C. Solving problems and making decisions in a business context
    1. Seeking and gathering information for business decisions
    2. Understanding the business context
    3. Understanding the societal/cultural context
    4. Seeing accounting as a coherent whole
    5. Using information for business decisions

D. Learning to be an independent learner
    1. Developing motivation
    2. Developing learning skills
    3. Developing information seeking skills

E. Developing broad perspectives
    1. Global perspectives
    2. Eethical perspectives
    3. Entrepreneurial perspectives

In this list of desired outcomes, as in the AECC profile of capabilities and the BYU list of competencies, accounting and business knowledge is only part of what the future accountant is seen to need. People skills, problem-solving skills, and developing broad perspectives are equally important. Learning to learn also appears as a significant goal of several change projects. The components of independent learning listed here— motivation, learning skills, information-seeking skills—reflect the emphases of different programs.

In these lists of desired outcomes and competencies, learning to learn is both stated as a separate goal and implied in the statements of other goals. Its importance is clear, but the concept itself is not. There is general agreement that future accounting professionals need to be lifelong, continuing, independent learners and that accounting programs should help them to become such learners. However, there is no clear consensus on what constitutes learning to learn, how to know when a student is doing it, how or when or even if learning to learn can be taught and learned. Accounting educators want to include learning to learn in their programs, but are uncertain about how to introduce it into the accounting curriculum.

Consequently, we will review several ways to look at learning to learn and propose a limited working definition of the concept. We will use this definition in this monograph and will suggest a process of learning that can readily be introduced into accounting courses and curricula. We propose this process as the beginning of what must become both for individuals and for the profession a continuous emphasis on learning.

## 1.2 Learning to Learn

Educators do not agree on one approach to the question of what is learning to learn. For example, learning to learn can be considered as a concept to be explored, an abstract theory to be tested and explained. It can also be considered as a goal of education, at any level from early childhood through adulthood. Or it can be considered as a process, an ongoing activity that permeates an educational program or an individual's lifestyle. Finally, it can be seen as product, the achievement of the goal, the result of the process.

As a _goal_ of education, learning to learn leads to conscious training in the classroom, explicit learning of skills, attitudes, approaches to knowledge. Such training can range from teaching a child to identify words and understand key sentences to helping an adult learn to take notes or monitor comprehension of new concepts. Learning to learn has been the conscious subject of introductory college courses in English, psychology, sciences, and other subjects in several institutions. For example, in a psychology course called "Learning to Learn," freshmen at The University of Michigan study cognitive psychology and practice applying its principles in their own learning experiences (McKeachie, Pintrich, and Lin, 1985). In this situation, learning strategies are successfully taught in conjunction with subject matter.

As a _process_ of education, learning to learn becomes a less visible but equally potent element in the classroom or other educational setting. This process may be transparent to the student but it will be carefully orchestrated by the teacher. It requires a deliberate teaching style that promotes the attitudes, abilities, and strategies of independent learning. It is suitable for any subject and is implicit in how the subject is approached by both teacher and student. For example, in an accounting principles course a student might be encouraged to ask why the debt-to-equity ratio is important to a potential shareholder, rather than being told to remember that it is important. The process of learning to learn leads the student to adopt habits of thought and learning that continue beyond a specific educational experience.

As a *product* of education, learning to learn becomes an essential element in the professional's life and work. The ultimate product is the mature professional who is committed to continuing personal growth and to lifelong development of professional knowledge. This person is able to make conscious use of learning strategies in order to discover and assimilate new knowledge and to generate solutions to new professional problems. For example, a beginning professional in an accounting firm will approach an unfamiliar assignment by consciously drawing on a repertoire of learning strategies to discover possible solutions to the problem and to decide on a course of action. This mature professional learner is the desired graduate of the accounting programs of the future.

While recognizing the several ways of looking at this subject, we have chosen to define learning to learn as a *process*. We see learning to learn as a dynamic activity that occurs in any setting, at all ages, and continues outside of and beyond formal education and professional responsibilities. We believe this definition will be useful to accounting educators who want to include learning to learn in their curricula.

**We define learning to learn as a process of acquiring, understanding, and using a variety of strategies to improve one's ability to attain and apply knowledge, a process which results from, leads to, and enhances a questioning spirit and a lifelong desire to learn.**

## 1.3 Perspectives on Learning to Learn

As indicated above, there are many ways of looking at learning to learn. We will review several to put our own approach into perspective. Many of the ideas mentioned here have informed the synthesis we are presenting in this monograph.

The field of adult education is a rich source for accounting faculty interested in learning. Adult educators frequently study the experiences and motivations of independent, lifelong learners. Accounting educators may adapt some principles of adult education to help accounting students prepare for a lifetime of learning on their own. Two recent studies in this area are particularly interesting for our purpose. Smith and Associates (1990) focused on learning to learn across the life span and discussed models, challenges and opportunities for learning in the information age. Candy (1991) reviewed the scope, practice, and potential of self-directed lifelong learning.

Robert Smith, the adult educator quoted early in this chapter, discussed learning to learn as a promising approach to both formal and informal education (1990). He pointed out how contexts, including the setting or institution, subject matter or discipline, and personal learning style can affect the learning to learn process. Smith suggested a number of activities for students learning to learn (Figure 1.3).

Candy, an internationally known adult educator at Queensland University, Australia, reviewed the theory and practice of self-direction for lifelong learning. He

---

**FIGURE 1.3**
Activities for Learning to Learn

Develop self awareness and learn to monitor and reflect on educational activities.
Become an active learner so you can control your learning activities.
Develop a broad repertoire of learning strategies.
Learn to adjust to different teaching methods and subjects.
Develop confidence and motivation as a learner.
Recognize and compensate for your own learning deficiencies.
Improve group inquiry and problem-solving skills.
Choose educational resources that fit your needs and abilities.

Adapted from Smith and Associates (1990), p. 4

---

described self-direction as both a process and a product of education. As a process, self-education can mean learner-control (as opposed to teacher-control) in formal instructional settings, or it can mean intentional self-education outside formal settings. As a product, self-direction can be personal autonomy, or it can be self-management or independence in directing one's learning activities. Candy's discussion of learner-control and self-management or independence in learning are particularly relevant for accounting educators.

Candy suggested that learner control of instruction can help students become the kind of independent self-educators that accounting professionals need to be. While there is no proof that learner control leads to better learning of subject matter, there is "some evidence that prolonged exposure to techniques of instruction that emphasize high degrees of learner control can increase people's competence at, and preference for, independent inquiry" (p. 223). Learner control may be introduced gradually during a course or curriculum as learners and teachers adapt to changing roles and expectations. The goal is to give students experiences that empower them to learn independently in school and in their professional work.

What Candy called self-management or autonomy in learning is essentially what accounting educators are calling independent learning. Candy suggested that learners may be autonomous in some subjects and not in others and that the degree of autonomy may vary as well. He argued that autonomous learning is content and context specific and that it requires learner confidence as well as competence. Accounting educators can conclude from Candy's discussion that they need to encourage learner-control and self confidence in the accounting curriculum and that they need to teach students to be independent learners of accounting. That is, students need to learn about learning in the context of accounting if they are to become lifelong independent learners in their profession.

Candy's profile of the autonomous learner (Figure 1.4) suggests many of the learning qualities desired for future accountants.

**FIGURE 1.4**
CANDY'S PROFILE OF AN AUTONOMOUS LEARNER

The autonomous/independent learner must be:
  1. Methodical/disciplined
  2. Logical/analytical
  3. Reflective/self aware
  4. Curious/motivated
  5. Flexible
  6. Interdependent/interpersonally competent
  7. Venturesome/creative
  8. Confident/positive
  9. Independent/self sufficient
The autonomous/independent learner must have:
  10. Information seeking and retrieval skills
  11. Knowledge about, and skills at, learning processes
  12. Ability to evaluate skills and progress, information and knowledge,
      problems and solutions.

Adapted from Candy (1991), pp. 459-466

The field of psychology is, of course, a fruitful source of information about learning to learn. In particular, cognitive psychology offers useful insights into the learning process. Bloom's taxonomy of cognitive objectives (Bloom, 1956) was developed to help faculty set course and program learning goals. It presents a hierarchy of cognitive skills that can be used to arrange learning activities in a logical sequence (Figure 1.5).

**FIGURE 1.5**
BLOOM'S TAXONOMY OF COGNITIVE OBJECTIVES

| | | |
|---|---|---|
| Knowledge | - | identifying and recalling information |
| Comprehension | - | selecting and using facts or ideas |
| Application | - | using facts, rules, theories, or principles in specific situations |
| Analysis | - | separating the whole into parts to see relationships and discover the structure of an idea or concept |
| Synthesis | - | combining parts or facts to develop new, creative ideas |
| Evaluation | - | developing opinions or making decisions on materials, information, or problem situations |

Accounting faculty at Kansas State University used Bloom's taxonomy in their AECC grant project on curriculum change. The new KSU curriculum emphasizes the cognitive skills of knowledge, comprehension, and application in early courses, and includes analysis, synthesis, and evaluation in advanced courses. For example, in Accounting Theory and History, juniors practice analysis and synthesis by considering alternative solutions to economic problems. In Accounting Research, seniors practice synthesis and evaluation as they learn to conduct research and solve complex professional problems (Ainsworth and Plumlee, 1993).

In a chapter called Teaching Students How to Learn (McKeachie, 1994), Weinstein describes independent learning as "strategic learning" which includes motivation, learning skills, and what Weinstein called executive control of the learning process. Accounting educators may find her analogy of an executive overseeing the learning process helpful. By executive control Weinstein means that students (1) organize and manage their own approach to learning; (2) monitor their progress toward the learning goal; and (3) develop a repertoire of effective learning strategies (p. 366). Weinstein suggests that faculty can help students by explaining how to approach new learning tasks, by modeling different learning strategies, and by encouraging students to take ownership of their goals and responsibility for their learning.

Weinstein's chapter appears in W. J. McKeachie's Teaching Tips, a very practical and readable introduction to the psychology of teaching and learning. Now in its ninth edition, the book offers many helpful insights for accounting educators interested in helping students learn to learn. Of particular interest to accounting faculty will be McKeachie's discussion of learning and cognition in the classroom, and motivating students for lifelong learning. McKeachie combines research, theory, and practice in his discussion of teacher roles and student learning.

The work of psychologists and adult educators, like that discussed here, suggests a number of themes important for the preparation of independent, lifelong learners. These include student motivation, goal setting, self-management of strategies and effort, individual responsibility, and an understanding of learning as a continuous process. Essentially, the studies call upon students to practice what psychologists call "metacognition," that is, to think about thinking, know about knowing, be aware of and control the learning process. These practices are basic to the ability to learn to learn.

## 1.4 Learning as a Professional Responsibility

Accounting is not alone in promoting a focus on learning to learn. Most professions expect their members to continue learning throughout their careers. However, what is envisioned in the new learning to learn emphasis is much more challenging to students than the continuing professional education often required today. Curriculum changes similar to those being proposed for accounting are being introduced into a number of professional programs.

A good example of this kind of change is the introduction of problem-based learning in medical education. Like accountants, physicians are faced with a rapidly expanding knowledge base and with difficult and complex professional problems. Traditionally, medical students have been trained in rigorous basic science courses involving large lectures, frequent exams, and the need to memorize volumes of information, followed by two or more years of clinical work. Now, some medical schools offer a problem-based learning program that includes group learning, tutorials, ethics seminars, and frequent contact with patients and practitioners. Medical students in these programs learn how to find and use information to solve health problems presented in written cases or by real patients. They develop the technical knowledge needed, but they also learn how to learn and how to work with patients and colleagues (Barrows and Tamblyn, 1980). Started on a limited scale by a few schools, problem-based learning is attracting wide attention among medical educators because it has been successful in developing medical students into active, involved learners.

Engineering is another field which is moving from a purely technical educational process to a more active teaching/learning approach. The engineering curriculum has traditionally been dominated by math, science, and technical subjects, but engineering practice calls also for skills in handling design, production, and management issues. Engineering schools are moving to integrate theory and practice in the curriculum and to include training in leadership, teamwork, communication, and interpersonal skills.

The concept of reflective practice developed by Donald Schon (1983, 1987) provides a theoretical base for the kinds of changes proposed for professional education, including accounting education. Schon, professor of Urban Studies and Planning at MIT, suggested that effective professional practice requires more than theoretical and applied knowledge; it requires good judgment and wise decisions in a variety of complex situations. Professional training, then, must include opportunities to apply and adapt knowledge and to reflect on practice as one engages in the process. Schon used architecture, music, and psychoanalytic practice as examples, but applied his concept also to law, medicine, and business.

Schon (1987) maintained that there is a "core of artistry" in the practice of very competent professionals, that this artistry is a way of "knowing-in-action" what to do, and that there are "an art of problem framing, an art of implementation, and an art of improvisation—all necessary to mediate the use in practice of applied science and techniques" (p. 13). To become effective professionals, students need to learn the artistry as well as the theory and techniques of their profession. This need creates the paradox of learning a new competence: "a student cannot at first understand what he needs to learn, can learn it only by educating himself, and can educate himself only by beginning to do what he does not yet understand" (p. 93).

Schon proposed the "reflective practicum" as an effective way to teach professionals the artistry of practice. In such a course, students learn by doing and by thinking about what they are doing, a process Schon called "reflection-in-action." Teachers coach students by modeling practice, raising questions, and offering suggestions and alternatives. We know from experience that such a course can work. A decade before Schon wrote, the senior author of this monograph was using many of the reflective practicum techniques in teaching writing to future teachers at a midwestern university. Her students learned by writing and by critiquing one another's work, while she coached them to produce writing better than she—or her students—could have done alone. The reflection-in-action process can work in any course where students need to practice what they are learning.

Schon described the primary activities of the reflective practicum as "learning by doing, coaching rather than teaching, and a dialogue of reciprocal reflection-in-action between coach and students" (p. 303). His students learned to become professionals by practicing in the safe environment of the practicum. However, not all students will be responsive at first to the demands of a reflective practicum. Some will resist suggestions, some will want to be told what to think or do. Accounting faculty who introduce reflection-in-action into their courses may need to convince their students that they can learn by doing as well as by memorizing accounting.

The concept of reflective practice informs our discussion of learning to learn in accounting education in two ways. First, as the studies we have reviewed make clear, reflection is an important element in learning to learn. Awareness, understanding, and thinking about the learning process are all essential to effective, independent learning. Second, what we might call reflective learning is clearly essential to the successful practice of most professions. This is why the AECC emphasizes that, "The overriding objective of accounting programs should be to teach students to learn on their own....Students should be taught the skills and strategies that help them learn more effectively and how to use these effective learning strategies to continue to learn throughout their lifetimes" (Objectives, p. 4). Like doctors, lawyers, engineers, and others, accountants are finding that learning-in-practice is an essential, continuing responsibility of a successful professional.

# Chapter Two
# INTENTIONAL LEARNING

Two contrasting views of the teaching-learning experience are common in higher education. One envisions the student as an empty vessel to be filled with academic content. In this vision the professor and content determine the nature of the course. Students are allowed—even encouraged—to be passive learners. The second view suggests that the student is an active participant in the learning which is the goal of the course. The professor facilitates the learning, organizes tasks and content to encourage learning, and helps the student evaluate his success. But student learning is at the center of the course. Both the process of learning and the course content determine what happens in the classroom.

In the second of these hypothetical classrooms, the student becomes an active, involved learner. He practices what we are calling intentional learning, that is, learning with self-directed purpose, intending and choosing that he will learn and how he will learn and what he will learn. This learner comes to his studies with professional purpose, raising questions, reflecting on answers and adapting what is learned to new situations and problems. Consciously practicing intentional learning in the classroom empowers this student to become the independent, lifelong learner needed by the accounting profession.

We present here intentional learning as a workable process that can be used by accounting professors and students to develop attitudes and skills for success in learning accounting. In this chapter we focus on the concept and attributes of intentional learning. In Chapter Three we will describe student characteristics that affect learning, and in Chapter Four we will suggest teaching strategies to introduce the attributes of learning into accounting courses. We believe that accounting faculty can use intentional learning to guide their introduction of learning to learn into the accounting curriculum.

## 2.1 Attributes of Intentional Learning

In discussing intentional learning, we use the word learner deliberately, to differentiate our student from the student who needs to be taught. The learner acts independently or with guidance that facilitates the acquisition of knowledge he wishes to attain. We suggest five attributes that are essential elements of intentional learning: questioning, organizing, connecting, reflecting, and adapting. These attributes are listed with short descriptions in Figure 2.1.

The five attributes described have been chosen to be as inclusive as possible but they are not a definitive list. They include what we consider to be the most important general abilities required to become an independent learner in any field. The five attributes permit us to focus our discussion on reasonably accessible ideas and activities. We suggest that accounting faculty adapt and use these attributes in their own

---

**FIGURE 2.1**
ATTRIBUTES OF INTENTIONAL LEARNING

QUESTIONING - facts, theories, experiences; wanting to learn; asking independent questions about what is to be known.
ORGANIZING - ideas, meaning, knowledge; developing understanding of what is learned.
CONNECTING - new knowledge with old; integrating what is learned into a broader pattern of understanding.
REFLECTING - on what and how and why one is learning; understanding one's learning needs and strategies.
ADAPTING - to new situations and needs; using what is learned in a changing world or profession.

---

courses as a way to encourage students to become independent learners. We believe that students who practice these attributes in accounting courses will be prepared to become lifelong independent learners in their accounting careers.

QUESTIONING is essential to effective learning. By questioning we mean going beyond superficial clarifications to profound wondering about what is to be known. The learner asks questions because he wants to know more and wants to probe beyond the obvious. His questions aim at meanings, not just simple answers. This attitude must be encouraged if he is to become an independent learner.

The questioning attribute has its basis in human curiosity. Most children naturally ask a lot of questions; as they grow older and more self-conscious they suppress their questions rather than risk appearing foolish. Motivation theory suggests that natural curiosity is an essential element in self-directed learning. Accounting educators should encourage their students to ask questions in order to develop a lifelong spirit of inquiry.

ORGANIZING is the second essential attribute of intentional learning. Most knowledge can be organized into structures; the field of accounting is one such structure. Effective learning involves organizing ideas, meaning, and knowledge into an orderly system. In this way the learner develops understanding of what is learned, and makes sense of the facts, concepts, principles he is acquiring. An educational program can help a learner see the relevant structures and practice organizing knowledge effectively.

The attribute of organizing is related to what educational psychologists call cognitive structures, that is, how students organize, represent, and construct meaning out of what they are learning. Cognitive structures help students understand and remember new information. Structures may be verbal (such as outlines) or visual (diagrams, models). Research suggests that students succeed best in courses where their cognitive structures most closely resemble those of their instructor (McKeachie et al., 1986). Accounting educators may find it helpful to share their own sense of the discipline with students, especially students new to accounting.

The attribute of CONNECTING involves integrating what is learned into a broader pattern of understanding. The learner connects new knowledge with what he already knows, enlarging and enhancing both the new and the old. Learning is not isolated or discrete, but is combined to produce new understandings. The learner sees or makes connections that give meaning to what he learns.

The connecting attribute has implications both for a student's general education and for his interest in learning. Some recent national reports on higher education have stressed the importance of integrating knowledge and of helping students connect what they are learning in different courses and outside of class (Association of American Colleges, 1990). In addition to broadening education by connecting ideas, students can be motivated to learn by making connections with experience—their own and others. Both kinds of connections help students understand and remember what they are learning.

REFLECTING on what, how, and why one is learning is another essential attribute of intentional learning. Reflecting introduces awareness of oneself as a learner. It means understanding one's learning needs and style, consciously acquiring a variety of learning strategies and deliberately choosing to use those strategies that will work most efficiently. Intentional learning involves reflective learning.

Research suggests that awareness of and reflection on the learning process is the essence of learning to learn. For example, Smith describes learning to learn as "an executive function of learning that serves to increase one's ability to manage the specifics of learning so that one is empowered to control more and more of the educational experience in one's own way, time and place" (1990, p. 67). The self-conscious management of the learning process Smith described can be achieved through the practice of reflecting on one's learning activities and achievements.

The attribute of ADAPTING includes elements of applying and implementing. It involves using what is learned in a changing world or profession. It means applying one's learning to professional practice, implementing knowledge in daily life, and adapting or changing what one has learned in order to meet new situations or challenges. Adapting implies flexibility and leads to creativity in developing new approaches to professional problems.

The term adapting derives from Stark's concept of adaptive competence, one of six professional competencies described in *Responsive Professional Education* (1986). Adaptive competence involves: "(1) sensing and detecting changing conditions in the internal or external environment that affect practice; (2) acknowledging the need to alter or adapt some mode of functioning; and (3) taking steps to initiate or accommodate the changes required...." (p. 48). The learner who asks questions, organizes ideas, connects new knowledge with old, and reflects on his own learning also adapts that learning to create solutions to the challenges of change.

## 2.2 The Intentional Learning Process

Seen in its broadest sense, learning begins with the physical experience of the infant, the incessant questions of the toddler, the reading, writing, arithmetic of elementary education. These early experiences provide the base for the learning process of the college student. The learner new to a field or subject studies facts and acquires knowledge. As his learning progresses, it becomes more complex and involves developing intellectual skills and understanding learning strategies. Eventually, the most successful learner applies learning to the issues and problems of personal and professional life. This individual practices intentional learning and becomes an independent learner.

Learning can be described as surface or deep, short-term or long-term. These descriptions are closely related and present a basic dichotomy. Surface/short-term learning focuses on information that is easily learned and easily forgotten. Deep/long-term learning focuses on the same kind of information but organizes it into meaningful knowledge that can be remembered and used when needed. Learning in many fields, including accounting, can also be described as development of skills used in practice or application of knowledge. The challenge for accounting educators is to help students move from surface learning of accounting rules to deep understanding of accounting principles and to skill in using knowledge in practice.

A given individual may be at different stages in developing as a learner, depending on the subject or task involved. For example, a college athlete could be intentional about studying baseball: reading and using baseball theory, reviewing the strengths and weaknesses of his opponents, practicing signals and inventing strategies. That same student could be a beginning learner in chemistry, where he studies facts, memorizes formulae, and reproduces this information on objective tests. And he could be a more sophisticated learner thinking critically in accounting classes, where he applies principles of accounting to problems at his workplace.

Our concept of intentional learning has been informed by psychologists who see the learning process as a continuum. McKeachie summarized this notion in a review of teaching/learning research:

> ....there is a continuum running from what is usually termed 'learning' to 'problem solving' and 'creativity.' We usually say that someone has learned when they display the effects of training or experience in a context similar to that in which the learning occurred. We talk about 'transfer of learning' when the learning is displayed in a situation somewhat different from that in which the original learning occurred. If the transfer situation is so different that the use of the learning encounters some barrier of difficulty, we speak of 'problem solving.' When the situation is greatly different and the distance of transfer needed is greater still, we speak of 'creativity' (McKeachie, et al., 1986, p. 33).

Although we began our work by thinking about learning to learn as a continuum, we developed the concept of intentional learning as both cumulative and cyclical. We see the process as moving from acquiring knowledge to developing intellectual skills to intentional learning. The learner who is intentional in one field may return to acquiring knowledge when he undertakes study of a different subject. The key to intentional learning is understanding the process and making conscious choices among a variety of strategies.

To envision the intentional learning process, we have developed the diagram presented as Figure 2.2. The diagram is intended only as a visual representation, not as a definitive explanation of key elements in the process. It is a device to help us and our readers see the steps students take as they learn and learn to learn.

The learning process is depicted here in three columns of increasing sophistication and intentionality. The process starts in the first column with information or knowledge. To attain knowledge, the learner acquires and practices a number of relatively

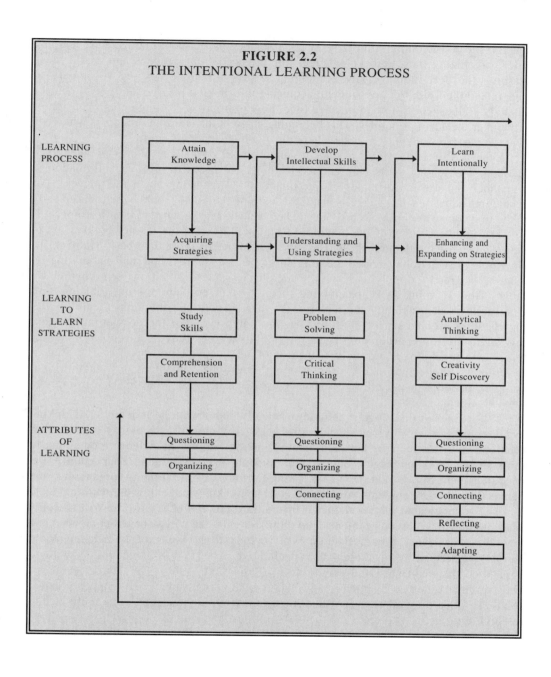

**FIGURE 2.2**
THE INTENTIONAL LEARNING PROCESS

LEARNING PROCESS

Attain Knowledge → Develop Intellectual Skills → Learn Intentionally

Acquiring Strategies → Understanding and Using Strategies → Enhancing and Expanding on Strategies

LEARNING TO LEARN STRATEGIES

Study Skills | Problem Solving | Analytical Thinking

Comprehension and Retention | Critical Thinking | Creativity Self Discovery

ATTRIBUTES OF LEARNING

Questioning | Questioning | Questioning

Organizing | Organizing | Organizing

| Connecting | Connecting

| | Reflecting

| | Adapting

unsophisticated learning strategies. The learner begins by memorizing facts, learning rules, organizing these into knowledge. For the accounting student, this could mean learning the definitions of key accounting terms so that he has the vocabulary to understand the field. For any student, acquiring information may go along with courses in study skills such as how to manage time, how to improve reading comprehension or remember facts and principles. This beginning stage in the learning process is where we find the passive student. It may be where most college students start.

Even at this early stage, a student can begin to develop attributes of intentional learning. The learner starts with surface learning, but needs to organize information to remember and use it. Attributes of questioning and organizing begin this process. For accounting educators, this suggests that these learning attributes should be introduced early in the first course as conscious activities to help students make sense of their learning.

The middle column of the diagram in Figure 2.2 shows the learner progressing to development of intellectual skills. Here the student needs more than basic study skills. He employs such sophisticated learning strategies as summarizing and elaborating on what he has read, or applying general principles to specific situations or problems. He moves from learning facts to applying them, first in problem solving (dealing with clearly defined problems and solutions), then in critical thinking (dealing with unstructured problems with multiple—or no—solutions). For the accounting student, this might mean preparing and discussing in class a case study of a troubled company that needs to improve the quality and use of its financial information. The student developing intellectual skills asks probing questions, organizes information into complex patterns, and begins to make connections between what he is learning and what he already knows.

The learner at this stage is thinking critically about what he is learning. Thinking and learning are closely related activities and psychologists are not agreed on their relationship or distinctions between them. Thinking requires knowledge (something to think about), but knowledge is not enough. Students need also practice, opportunity, and encouragement to think on their own. Using attributes of questioning, organizing, and connecting can help students think about and use the knowledge they are learning.

The sophisticated learner depicted in the third column of Figure 2.2 will not only acquire knowledge, solve problems, and think critically, he will also reflect on what and how he is learning. This reflection will include three kinds of knowledge about learning, described by psychologists as declarative (what to do), procedural (how to do it), and conditional (when and why to do it) (Paris et al., 1983). This learner enhances his learning strategies by practicing analytical thinking and by developing creative solutions to learning problems. At this stage an accounting student will be motivated to research a problem, explore a number of solutions, and propose a direction to follow. He will be prepared to reflect on how he is finding solutions and to adapt what he is learning to other new situations.

As the learner moves through the intentional learning process, his learning skills become more sophisticated and more self conscious. That is, questions probe more deeply, organization becomes more complex, connections become more clear and logical. Evaluation of progress is crucial to this development. Accounting faculty should include evaluation of the quality and use of the attributes of learning when they introduce questioning, organizing, etc., into their courses. They will find Gainen and Locatelli's

AECC assessment guide (1995) a helpful resource. The guide offers many suggestions, including a chart on assessing the five attributes which we have reproduced as Appendix C. Ultimately, an experienced, independent learner will include self-evaluation in his reflections on learning. Faculty can help learners develop self-evaluation skills by emphasizing improvement and evaluation of the attributes of learning.

Although the intentional learning process is depicted in Figure 2.2 in three columns of increasing sophistication, the process is cyclical as well as cumulative. Learners build on previous skills as they move through the process. Thus the process echoes Bloom's hierarchical taxonomy of cognitive objectives and McKeachie's image of a learning continuum. But we also see the process as continuing and cyclical, the learner returning to the first stages to attain more knowledge and develop more intellectual skills in connection with a new topic. For example, an accounting student could practice all the attributes of intentional learning by the end of intermediate accounting courses, and then be expected to use with conscious attention the activities of attaining knowledge in a graduate international tax course. Because he understands the process, this learner will be able to move quickly to problem solving and analytical thinking, that is, to adapting and using previous experience of intentional learning.

## 2.3 Encouraging Intentional Learning

Content-oriented courses dominate many American colleges and universities. Many faculty feel compelled to cover more and more material. Many students feel overwhelmed by the quantity of information presented to them. Under these circumstances, learning becomes a matter of managing the workload. This has been particularly true for accounting education as the profession has changed. It is well recognized that "covering" a lot of material does not ensure either student attention or retention, and under these circumstances, questioning, connecting, reflecting, and adapting become practically impossible.

Encouraging intentional learning requires moving away from this scenario and toward a classroom that involves students both in the content and in the learning process. This involvement means not just employing intentional learning strategies in class, but also helping students to reflect on those strategies and how they are used. Since most professors do not have expertise in learning theory, it is easier for them simply to focus on what is to be learned and hope that their students either have the attributes of intentional learning or will develop them without direct help. It is also easier for students to remain passive absorbers of content than to involve themselves actively in learning. The challenge then for the accounting professor is to balance her course between focus on the content to be covered and on the process of learning it. This balance will vary from course to course and will not be easy to find, but it is essential to achieving the goals of learning to learn.

Complicating the task of seeking balance is the false perception that student learning characteristics are immutable. As many successful faculty know, student learning styles, goals, and motivations can evolve as faculty encourage students to learn intentionally. Faculty can adopt teaching strategies and model learning processes that can influence student learning abilities. For example, the psychology course at The University of Michigan that specifically teaches learning strategies has been shown to improve students' knowledge and use of varied strategies. Course results included a reduction in test-taking anxieties and modest improvement in grades (McKeachie, Pintrich, and Lin, 1985). A similar course at the University of Texas teaches students about learning and offers practice in a variety of learning techniques. Students make substantial gains in reading comprehension, in performance on a variety of learning tasks, and in their grade point averages (Weinstein and Underwood, 1985).

At some institutions, separate courses in learning to learn are offered, especially to beginning or underprepared students. These courses can be useful in training students to use particular study skills or to be more aware of their own learning processes. However, in order to make learning meaningful, the content of the learning must be important to the learner. We believe that accounting courses in the new curriculum should include attention to both accounting content and the process of learning. We recognize that this presents a difficult challenge for accounting faculty, but we believe that using the intentional learning model will help them meet that challenge.

Faculty cannot, however, expect to be totally successful with all students. It appears that students who lack basic reading and number skills do not benefit much from exposure to new learning strategies. Research also suggests that students need a certain level of maturity for truly effective learning. The learning task and evaluation methods also affect the learning process; a student who is expected only to "absorb content" and who knows he will be taking a multiple-choice test will concentrate on memorizing facts rather than on applying broad principles. Finally, students need to find ways to transfer learning abilities from one content area to another. Some research has been done on this, but more needs to be done.

Most students can be helped to develop the attributes of intentional learning. Accounting professors who want to encourage these attributes should consider the characteristics of their students that either help or hinder the learning process. Chapter three will point out characteristics that are important to the learning process and suggest ways to take these into consideration in course planning. Accounting professors can adopt a number of teaching strategies that will promote the learning process without detracting seriously from attention to accounting content. By attending to learner needs and promoting the attributes of intentional learning, the accounting professor can encourage students to learn to learn efficiently and well.

---

### LEARNING ABOUT LEARNING

We suggest three easily accessible sources for faculty to learn about learning.

1. Ask students to describe critical incidents in their own learning experience or to keep a learning journal which you can review periodically (see Stephen Brookfield, *The Skillfull Teacher,* for suggestions).

2. Reflect on your own biography as a learner: what courses and teachers do you remember and why? What motivates you to keep learning today?

3. Regularly read one or more of the journals that focus on teaching or student learning. Choices for accounting faculty might include: *Issues in Accounting Education, The Journal of Accounting Education, College Teaching, The Teaching Professor* (newsletter).

# Chapter Three
# INDIVIDUAL CHARACTERISTICS
# THAT INFLUENCE LEARNING

Accounting faculty need to know about their students as well as about their subject and how to teach it. In this chapter we review a number of individual characteristics that influence a student's learning. While not an exhaustive survey, the chapter presents what we consider to be the salient characteristics that influence the attributes of questioning, organizing, connecting, reflecting, and adapting knowledge.

We begin by describing personal characteristics, some of which (age, gender, and socioeconomic background) cannot be changed. We then discuss some developmental characteristics that have been shown to be important in moral and intellectual maturity. We also discuss learning styles and how they can be improved. Finally, we discuss how motivation and goals can influence the quality and outcomes of the learning experience. We include information about the characteristics of accounting students that should be considered as we seek to help them become effective learners.

## 3.1 Personal Characteristics

A recent article in *Change* magazine (Schroeder, 1993) begins with a familiar scene: faculty complaining about students in college today. The senior professor summarizes the problem, "I tell you one thing, my classroom would be a much better place if students were more like me!" The truth is, the majority of students today are not like their professors, and not at all like the students their professors remember themselves to have been. The composition of the American student body has changed significantly since most faculty were in school.

These changes have occurred in several basic student characteristics. Most obvious is gender; today over 50% of college students are women. Another factor is age; more than one-third of today's college students are over 25 years of age. A third factor is increased ethnic diversity on campus. Today more than 16% of college students are non-white, and that percentage will continue to grow. U.S. Census Bureau projections indicate that by the year 2000 more than 30% of 18-24 year-olds in the population will be members of minority groups.

In a typical accounting class today, over half the students are women. Growth in accounting enrollments from the 1960's into the mid 1980's came almost entirely from an influx of women. Doyle Williams, former chair of the AECC, predicts that the gender mix will level off at about 40% men, 60% women. Very often, women will be among the top students in the class. A number of studies have shown that women typically and consistently earn better grades in accounting classes than do their male peers.

Because an increasing proportion of American 18-year-olds will be from minority groups, accounting programs will need to attract and retain minority students. Today, only one percent of CPA's are black, and their ranks are not growing. Yet a Gallup/AICPA study showed 47% of black college students expressed interest in an accounting career (AICPA, 1991).

A recent study on the effect of race, gender, and expectations showed that majority students have higher expectations of success in introductory accounting than minority students do. In fact, the majority students do achieve more success in this course. Minority students, especially black males, are far more likely to drop introductory accounting than are majority students (Carpenter, Friar, and Lipe, 1993). Some minority students may lack adequate academic preparation; others may be discouraged by lack of encouragement or by coursework that does not connect with their own experience. If accounting programs are to build on minority interest in the profession, they will need to find ways to retain these students in the first course. Some possible steps might be academic skills enhancement, curricular changes (more time, more relevant examples and problems, bridging courses), and exposure to role models such as minority practitioners.

Another demographic influence on accounting education is the growth of two-year colleges and the numbers of transfer students. Significant numbers of accounting students take the first accounting course and much of their general education coursework at a two-year college. In fact, it is likely that a majority of accounting principles courses are taught at two-year schools. The result may be a variety of skill levels and background in the upper-division courses at many four-year schools. Recognizing this phenomenon, the AECC has published its Issues Statement No. 3 on the importance of two-year colleges for accounting education. The statement stresses the need for cooperation between two-year and four-year schools in order to improve accounting education.

The quality of accounting students is another characteristic of great concern to faculty. There is some evidence that accounting is not attracting the top students. In the Gallup/AICPA poll, high school high achievers indicated less interest in accounting than did their less talented schoolmates. College high achievers and students from highly selective schools were much less likely to major in business than were lower achieving students. A study sponsored by Coopers & Lybrand found that accounting majors had lower average SAT scores than did other majors. Students who had always been accounting majors had lower scores than did students who transferred into the major. Also, freshmen planning to major in accounting were likely to be attending colleges of medium or low selectivity, another indication of low SAT scores (Inman, Wenzler, and Wickert, 1989). While test scores and academic achievement are not the only possible measures of quality, they are partial indicators of students' readiness to become effective learners.

The "traditional" college student enrolls directly from high school at about age 18, attends a four-year college full time, lives on campus, and enjoys the support of her family. The new majority college student is older, has been out of school for some time, has a job, family responsibilities, and is enrolled part-time. This "new" student may be deeply committed to education, but other responsibilities often interfere with learning. Accounting faculty should consider these students' needs when planning coursework and requirements. For example, most part-time students spend very little time on campus, rushing from class to work or to meet family responsibilities. Faculty who assign group work could allot a few minutes of class time for groups to organize themselves; faculty who assign library work could consider the resources of nearby public libraries as well as campus facilities; faculty who assign computer work could ask· administrators for extended laboratory hours or could make the assignments amenable to a variety of equipment so students could work at home or at their business.

Helping today's college students to become effective learners is a significant challenge for accounting faculty. Some students are in school to accumulate credits and acquire a credential; they need to understand the importance of learning. Some students want to learn but lack confidence in their ability to do so; they will need support and encouragement. Most students need help organizing their efforts and seeing relationships among different courses and between coursework and their personal lives and aspirations. To help these students learn to learn, faculty may need to discuss the attributes of intentional learning and encourage students to make deliberate efforts to practice them.

Many college students today will have questions, but lack confidence to ask. Faculty can encourage student questioning by pointing out the role of questioning in learning to learn. Many students will have developed patterns of organizing ideas that are not suitable for academic material. Faculty may need to spend time at the beginning of a course to help students see the structure of the discipline in order to make sense of what they are learning. Faculty also need to take student experience seriously, to help students make connections between their lives and what they are learning in class. Busy students with many responsibilities are not likely to have much experience with reflecting. Faculty need to encourage them to take time to reflect on what and how they are learning, so that they can mature as learners. Students who are already working may find it easier to practice adapting than do younger students who are looking forward to employment. Faculty can encourage mature students to discuss their work experience and to apply concepts from class to their work environment.

Accounting and other faculty can develop a variety of pedagogical approaches to meet the needs of a diverse student population. A number of suggestions will be offered in the next chapter. Successful faculty will take time to learn something about the personal characteristics of their students, and will consider those characteristics when planning a course.

## 3.2 Intellectual Development

In almost every introductory accounting class, there is at least one student who insists on being told the right answer and who resists any suggestion that there might be more than one answer to a question or problem. In the same class, almost inevitably, will be another student who denies that any answer can be superior to any other answer; to this student, any opinion is good if you can support it. These two students represent two different stages or levels of intellectual development commonly found in college classes. They may be equally bright and competent, but their intellectual development will significantly influence these students' ability to become mature, independent learners.

An abundant amount of research over the past twenty-five years has explored the question of intellectual development in college. This research has led to general agreement about the direction of development and the elements of thought and behavior involved. Essentially these elements are: the nature of knowledge as perceived by the knower, the means of evaluating knowledge, the role of the learner, her peers, and the teacher. A student's perception of these elements affects how and what she learns.

Research shows that in college most students move through several stages of intellectual development. Their coursework and other college experiences can help them move through these stages. We will review briefly several studies of intellectual development and will suggest how a consideration of student intellectual development may help faculty shape accounting classes that help students learn effectively and mature intellectually.

William G. Perry Jr. interviewed students at Harvard and Radcliffe Colleges in the 1950's and 1960's to learn how they perceived the nature of knowledge, values, and responsibility. He found a clear pattern of development that included nine positions, from basic duality which sees the world as right versus wrong, true or false (the first student in our example above), to multiplicity and relativism which sees a variety of possible answers but still expects some absolutes to exist (our second student), and finally to commitment within a relativistic world in which one's affirmations are open to review and change. Perry saw the shift from relativism toward commitment as the most difficult for students and for their teachers. He suggested that students at this point need support from faculty who can share their own searches for meaning and make the students feel part of a community of searchers. Most of Perry's students were in the middle positions of his scheme, struggling with questions about the nature of truth, the role of authority (books or teachers), and the evaluation and use of knowledge (Perry, 1970.)

Most of Perry's subjects were young men. In several studies of women, Belenky and associates found both similarities and differences with Perry's scheme. The basic pattern of intellectual development was similar, from received knowledge which is concrete, dualistic, and focused on the one, right answer, through subjective knowledge which looks inward for answers, to procedural knowledge which uses formal methods to examine a complex world. The final perspective in Belenky's study is constructed knowledge which sees truth in the context of a complex, ambiguous world.

A particularly useful gender-related difference found in the Belenky study is the distinction between separate and connected knowing. Separate knowing (more characteristic of males) focuses on formal analysis of the object, person, topic under study; connected knowing (more characteristic of females) focuses on personal understanding of the topic or person to be known. Separate learning utilizes competition, debate, logical reasoning—approaches that separate self from the subject or ideas. Connected learning emphasizes cooperation, discussion, listening to and clarification of the ideas of others—approaches that involve learners with the subject and one another. Belenky proposes a style of "connected teaching" which believes in students, listens to them, and encourages their intellectual growth and development. (Belenky et al., 1986.)

Kitchener and King examined the intellectual development of college men and women from a perspective they called reflective judgment. Like Perry and Belenky, they found a pattern of development from a belief that knowledge is absolutely certain to a view that knowledge is completely uncertain and finally to a position that accepts some knowledge as more certain or true than other knowledge, but remains open to reexamining all claims. They found that students in the first or absolute stage could not distinguish between well-structured and ill-structured problems; these students believed that all problems have clear, simple answers. Most of the students in the Kitchener and King studies were in early (absolute) or middle (uncertain) stages of development.

Many faculty overestimated the intellectual maturity of their students, creating the potential for dissonance between teaching strategies and learning readiness. (King, Kitchener and Wood, 1985; King, Wood and Mines, 1990.)

Particularly useful for the purposes of this discussion is Marcia Baxter Magolda's analysis of student development and academic experience. She, too, found students moving from *dualism/certainty/absolute* knowing through *transition/uncertainty/ multiplicity* to what she called *independent* knowing and then, generally after graduation, to *contextual* knowing. Baxter Magolda interviewed college men and women over five years to trace their epistemological and intellectual development and to explore the effects of certain academic experiences on their growth and development. Because we feel that her work has especially useful implications for accounting faculty, we present some detail here. Figure 3.1 depicts Baxter Magolda's findings and provides a model of the basic pattern of student development (Baxter Magolda, 1992).

Baxter Magolda's work has the advantage of approximate balance in the gender of students interviewed. Like Perry and Belenky, she found that only a few students reached the final step, what she called the contextual pattern of knowing (2% of seniors, 12% of fifth year interviews). Freshmen were primarily (about 70%) absolute knowers, with the rest transitional. Sophomores were about evenly divided between absolute and transitional knowing; most juniors and seniors practiced transitional knowing. The independent pattern of knowing appeared in 16% of senior interviews and 57% of fifth year interviews, suggesting significant growth in these pivotal years. Baxter Magolda's findings suggest that accounting faculty whose students are most likely to be juniors and seniors can expect to find the majority of their students using the transitional pattern of knowing. Accounting courses can support students in their uncertainty and challenge them to move toward independent knowing.

In addition to describing the patterns of knowing, Baxter Magolda offers suggestions for teaching. For example, independent knowers want to be evaluated on their expression of their own ideas, a skill clearly important for accounting professionals. The following excerpt from a senior interview shows one student's response to an evaluation technique and typifies the material Baxter Magolda presents (p. 144):

> "Things were evaluated by how you explained yourself. It's essay questions. If you'd come up with a completely wrong answer, a wrong answer compared to what the teacher thought and you came up with a good idea about how to back it, then you would get credit for it. The answer wasn't the main thing; it was how you explained it."

Accounting faculty who want to promote independent, intentional learning may well start by considering the relationship between how they teach and evaluate students and the intellectual development of those students.

A comparison of Baxter Magolda's model and our diagram of the intentional learning process (Figure 2.2) reveals similar patterns of intellectual growth. The process of learning—attaining knowledge, developing intellectual skills, and learning intentionally—mirrors Baxter Magolda's developmental stages of absolute, transitional, independent, and contextual knowing. In both processes, students move systematically through the steps (that is, they don't jump from absolute to independent knowing

## FIGURE 3.1
## BAXTER MAGOLDA'S EPISTEMOLOGICAL REFLECTION MODEL

| Domains | Absolute Knowing | Transitional Knowing | Independent Knowing | Contextual Knowing |
|---|---|---|---|---|
| Role of learner | • Obtains knowledge from instructor | • Understands knowledge | • Thinks for self <br> • Shares views with others <br> • Creates own perspective | • Exchanges and compares perspectives <br> • Thinks through problems <br> • Integrates and applies knowledge |
| Role of peers | • Share materials <br> • Explain what they have learned to each other | • Provide active exchanges | • Share views <br> • Serve as a source of knowledge | • Enhance learning via quality contributions |
| Role of instructor | • Communicates knowledge appropriately <br> • Ensures that students understand knowledge | • Uses methods aimed at understanding <br> • Employs methods that help apply knowledge | • Promotes independent thinking <br> • Promotes exchange of opinions | • Promotes application of knowledge in context <br> • Promotes evaluative discussion of perspectives <br> • Student and teacher critique each other |
| Evaluation | • Provides vehicle to show instructor what was learned | • Measures students' understanding of the material | • Rewards independent thinking | • Accurately measures competence <br> • Student and teacher work toward goal and measure progress |
| Nature of knowledge | • Is certain or absolute | • Is partially certain and partially uncertain | • Is uncertain— everyone has own beliefs | • Is contextual; judge on basis of evidence in context |

without passing through a transitional phase). The roles of learner and teacher at the different stages of knowing are consistent with the learning to learn tasks of the student who is at the comparable point in the intentional learning process. For example, in the absolute knowing stage, the role of the learner is to obtain knowledge while the role of the teacher is to communicate knowledge and assure student understanding. These roles are comparable to the first column of Figure 2.2 where the learner concentrates on acquiring knowledge and practices questioning and organizing. Without pushing the comparison to extremes, we can see that the developmental process and the intentional learning process can work together to produce mature, independent learners.

---

### LEARNING AND KNOWING

Absolute Knower:
"The factual information is cut and dried. It is either right or wrong. If you know the information, you can do well. It is easy because you just read or listen to a lecture about the ideas. Then you present it back to the teacher."
Jim (p. 77)

Transitional Knower:
"The debate and discussion process for me is really interesting; I learn a lot more because I remember questions. And I guess I learn the most when I sit and I'm actually forced to raise my hand and then I have to talk. I have to sit there and think on the spot. I learn it better than in a note-taking class that is regurgitation."
Scott (p. 126)

Independent Knower:
"Case studies, group discussions, learning to interact with other people—I think that really helped you make your own decisions instead of spitting out facts that somebody has told you to memorize. You really make your own decisions, and you think subjectively and objectively about things, and you decide what you want to do and what you think about that."
Valerie (p. 159)

Contextual Knower:
"One independent study was this group idea of a reading group. The instructor didn't force himself into the picture but was always available if we wanted to come talk to him. Instead, we just got together and talked amongst ourselves. In that way, it wasn't divorced from your everyday intellectual life. And so, at the end of the course, you didn't feel as if 'Oh, I have to have this answer.' It was more or less how does this knowledge plug in to what I've learned here?"
Mark (p. 177)

Baxter Magolda, *Knowing and Reasoning in College*

We turn now to some applications of developmental theory to accounting education. In a prophetic article in 1984, Jean C. Wyer (an accountant who also holds an advanced degree in education) suggested that attention to developmental characteristics could be the key to reforming accounting education. She reviewed the then current debate between procedural and conceptual content in upper level accounting courses and suggested that the debate be broadened to include pedagogy as well as content. Wyer applied Perry's scheme to accounting education goals, including ethical and interpersonal as well as intellectual and content goals. She concluded that the goals for accounting education must "reflect the desired developmental results and....recognizing that the issues are related to pedagogical variables as well as content ones....[these goals] may also allow for the congenial marriage of all the requirements for entry into the profession with those for continuing beyond the entry level" (p. 15). Wyer interpreted the debate about accounting education as a debate between dualism and commitment and relativism. She saw that both students and faculty are often more comfortable with dualism and "the security that a closed, authoritative posture offers" (p. 17). Wyer's article suggests that accounting faculty should consider developmental level and growth as well as content in planning accounting courses. This means knowing where students are and then finding ways to help them make progress in their development.

The studies described here all seem to agree that while many freshmen enter college as dualistic/absolute knowers, most college students spend most of their college years in the multiplicity/transitional knowing stage. For example, Baxter Magolda's study included fourth-year interviews with 80 students. Of those 80, only 8 had reached the independent learning stage as seniors. Perry, Belenky and others found similar results. Even many adult students have been found to be predominantly in the transitional knowing stage as learners. In addition, students may slip back and forth from one stage to another depending on how comfortable they are with the material being studied. Faculty may infer student development by matching their observations of students against the attitudes about instruction, evaluation, and the nature of knowledge depicted in Figure 3.1 or any of the other schemes described here. We suggest that accounting faculty become familiar with one or more of these schemes so that they may recognize the developmental level of their students.

To help students mature as learners, faculty need to do more than provide content in courses. The studies cited here all suggest that faculty can be most effective if they provide both challenges and support geared to the students' developmental needs. The challenges force the student to try a different perspective; the support minimizes the student's risk in trying to move to the next stage of development. In a paper commissioned for a conference for accounting faculty, Rodgers offered a number of very specific suggestions for applying the developmental perspective to accounting courses. He used the example of a sophomore accounting assignment and suggested how to redesign the assignment for different developmental perspectives. Drawing on his ideas, we suggest a matrix such as the one below to help plan effective learning activities for intellectual development. (See Rodgers in Frecka, 1992 for more examples.)

Another paper commissioned for the same conference made direct connections between developmental perspectives and the new goals of accounting education. Joanne

**FIGURE 3.2**
**PLANNING MATRIX-STUDENT DEVELOPMENT**

|  | Dualistic/Absolute Knower | Relativist/Transitional Knower |
|---|---|---|
| Challenges: | present 2-3 conflicting views or explanations | evaluate 2-3 different points of view |
|  | use a process that emphasizes differences, not similarities | use a process that involves both differentiation and integration |
| Supports: | high degree of structure provided by instructor | let students structure their own learning |
|  | an open, encouraging atmosphere in class | class atmosphere encourages exchange of ideas with peers as well as isntructor |

Gainen, an expert on critical thinking, reviewed the AECC goals outlined in *Perspectives on Education* in the context of the work of Perry and Belenky. She pointed out that "students who are attracted to accounting because they believe it to be relatively free of uncertainty, 'cut-and-dried' and 'objective,' with procedures and principles to be memorized and applied algorithmically, reflect the developmental perspective of dualism/received knowledge. This perspective is not compatible with the attainment of educational goals outlined in *Perspectives*. A curriculum that aspires to foster complex intellectual skills must confront and seek to modify such students' dualistic beliefs about the field" (Frecka, p. 141).

Gainen suggested a number of instructional approaches that would help accounting students develop mature intellectual skills. For example, a model of informative testing which includes a mini test taken individually and again with a small group (both grades count) forces students to learn on their own, test their knowledge, and then share their ideas with their peers. The instructor structures the assignments and tests, discusses issues and problem questions, and lectures on key concepts and principles that the students have already studied. Another model, called cooperative controversy, involves groups of students in developing both intellectual and interpersonal skills. Working in groups of four, pairs of students study and present to their partner pair a position on a controversial subject. Then they switch sides, study, and present the other side of the argument. Each student writes a paper stating and supporting her final position on the subject. This approach offers both challenges and support to students who are beginning to become relativistic thinkers.

It should be clear from this brief discussion that a student's ability to learn intentionally, that is, her readiness to question, organize, connect, reflect on and adapt knowledge, depends heavily on her developmental position. Faculty should not expect a student to succeed on assignments that are beyond her level of intellectual development. For example, an absolute knower could be pushed to consider and question several different views of an issue rather than settling comfortably on one easy answer, but she should not be pressed to take a stand on one of those views. Once the student abandons her insistence on absolute/dualistic thinking and moves clearly into the transitional phase of uncertainty/multiplicity, she can be asked to reflect on several perspectives and to make at least a tentative commitment to one theory or solution. Accounting students need to move rather quickly from dualistic thinking to uncertainty/multiplicity in order to understand the complexity of their subject. Knowledge of student developmental characteristics should help accounting faculty plan sequences of topics and courses that help students move through the stages of intellectual development.

The developmental perspective may also help faculty plan effective teaching strategies for different students. Baxter Magolda studied student academic experiences and offered suggestions for effectively teaching absolute, transitional, independent, and contextual knowers. Absolute knowers appreciated "interesting activities" in class, by which they generally meant demonstrations by the teacher or opportunities to ask questions. They valued clear explanations and a supportive, encouraging class atmosphere. Transitional knowers appreciated student involvement, by which they meant group projects, applying their learning, doing something themselves (experiments, student teaching), and formulating their own theories. Independent knowers also valued involvement, but for different reasons. They wanted to involve both faculty and peers in mutual exploration of a variety of views. Contextual knowers looked for a collegial relationship with professors and fellow learners.

Several of the developmental schemes discussed here describe gender-related differences in learning styles. Belenky and associates described these as the connected style (mostly females) and the separate style (mostly males). Baxter Magolda found similar differences but broke them down even further. She described differences under each major kind of knowing as follows:

|          | Absolute  | Transitional  | Independent      |
|----------|-----------|---------------|------------------|
| (female) | receiving | interpersonal | interindividual  |
| (male)   | mastering | impersonal    | individual       |

As her terms suggest, Baxter Magolda found men's styles more individual or separate, women's more interpersonal or connected. It is important to remember, however, that not all men use one style and all women the other, nor does one person use one all the time. These are tendencies or preferences. However, in view of the increasing numbers of women in accounting classes, some attention should be paid to these differences. Accounting faculty might adapt assignments to accommodate different approaches at different points in the term. For example, debate is an effective approach for the separate learning style, but cooperative group work is more compatible with the connected style. An assignment might be structured to use groups to prepare for a debate, thus accommodating both approaches.

Teaching with attention to the students' developmental perspective does make a difference. Kurfiss reported several experiments in which courses were taught from a particular developmental perspective. Students in sections that matched their developmental perspective made more progress toward the next developmental position than did students who were mismatched. The course was designed to challenge students in a supportive way (Kurfiss, 1988). Accounting faculty can assume that typical students in the introductory course will be dualist/absolutist knowers. While they are not ready to be independent knowers, they can be nudged toward transitional knowing. The instructor can help them to see and accept the possibility of several truths, for example, by introducing some problems with more than one "right" answer. Accounting courses that challenge students in a supportive way can help them move toward the independent and contextual knowing that characterize intentional learning.

## 3.3 Learning Styles

Most people are aware that they have some preferred ways to approach a learning task, that others approach learning in other ways, and that no one way is best for every task and every person. Familiarity with some of the research on learning styles may help students identify their preferences and their strengths and weaknesses as learners. This awareness is an essential element in the process of learning to learn.

In spite of much research on the subject, there is no single, clearly agreed upon definition of learning style. Nor is there agreement on the relationship between learning style and intellectual development. For our purposes, we consider learning style to be how a student prefers to approach a learning task. We will review some research on learning style and suggest some ways this material may be useful to accounting educators.

Research suggests that students learn best when the teaching style is congruent with their learning style. Yet both students and faculty are almost certain to encounter courses where their styles are not congruent. Awareness on the part of both faculty and students could improve communication between them. Students can learn to adjust their approaches to learning when necessary; faculty can plan a variety of assignments to accommodate some of the learning style differences in a class. Both can attend to the process of learning as well as to the content.

A useful introduction to the subject of learning styles is Claxton and Murrell's *Learning Styles: Implications for Improving Educational Practices* (1987). They use the image of an onion to describe four "layers" of research on learning styles. We have modified their image to show in Figure 3.3 a series of concentric circles depicting a framework of learning style research. The center circle contains a number of models that describe personality types; next come a series of models of how people process information; then a layer of social-interaction models; and finally, the outer layer contains instructional-preference models. The center or core, personality traits, is generally quite stable; the other layers are more amenable to change. That is, students are more likely to change or adjust their preference for style of instruction than they are to change their preferred mode of processing information or their basic personality characteristics. We will describe one example from each circle to suggest what kinds of insights might be gained from learning styles research.

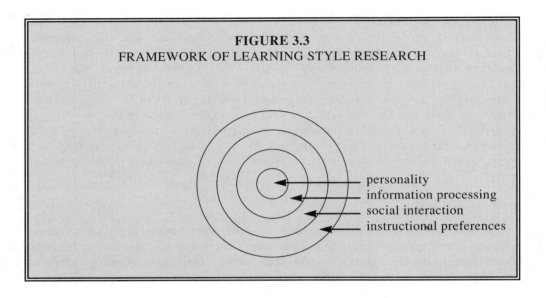

**FIGURE 3.3**
FRAMEWORK OF LEARNING STYLE RESEARCH

personality
information processing
social interaction
instructional preferences

The center circle of the framework contains research that describes personality types or character traits. One of the most widely known and used analyses of personality is the Myers-Briggs Type Indicator (MBTI), based on Jungian psychology. It examines how the individual perceives the world and makes decisions, using scores on four scales:

Extraversion/Introversion (E-I)
Sensing/Intuition (S-N)
Thinking/Feeling (T-F)
Judging/Perception (J-P)

An MBTI score will include four scales and is characterized by four letters indicating the preferences on each score, for example, ESFJ. Extraversion means a person relates most easily to the active world of people and things; introversion means the person prefers the reflective, inner world of ideas. Sensing suggests a preference for facts and concrete experience while intuition means the person looks for abstract possibilities and theories. Thinking means a person makes decisions based on analysis and logic while feeling means the person relies more on personal values. Judging reveals a preference for an orderly, planned way of life while perceptive suggests a more flexible, spontaneous approach to life. No one combination can be considered to be better than any other, though each type has its strengths and weaknesses.

In "New Students - New Learning Styles," Schroeder (1993) summarized some current studies of students and faculty using MBTI typology. He combined some MBTI scales to describe four patterns of learning:

ES - Extraversion/Sensing = concrete active
IS - Introversion/Sensing = concrete reflective
EN - Extraversion/Intuitive = abstract active
IN - Introversion/Intuitive = abstract reflective

Schroeder reported that about 50% of high school seniors exhibit the ES pattern, about 10% are IN, and the rest are about evenly divided between IS and EN. In the first year or two of college, these students are not equally successful. The IN students get the best test scores and the best grades as freshmen; the ES students get the lowest freshman grades and test scores. By junior year the two groups are doing equally well in their courses. Schroeder suggested that the practical-minded, concrete active ES students are more comfortable as juniors enrolled in their major and in courses they consider relevant and practical.

Based on Myers-Briggs data collected on faculty at many institutions over many years, Schroeder described faculty as very different from their students. In general, the majority of faculty prefer the IN (abstract reflective) learning style; less than 10% prefer the ES pattern that predominates among students. The result can be a mismatch in the classroom. "Concrete active (ES) learners come to class seeking direct, concrete experience, moderate-to-high degrees of structure, and a linear approach. They value the practical and the immediate, and the focus of their perception is primarily on the physical world. Their IN instructors, on the other hand, prefer the global to the particular, are stimulated by the realm of concepts, ideas, and abstractions, and assume that students, like themselves, need a high degree of autonomy in their work." (p. 25)

Accounting faculty and students could use Myers-Briggs results as a basis for discussion of teaching and learning styles and needs. The instrument could be offered to a class and the results discussed either by the accounting professor or by student services personnel. A student who knows she prefers a concrete active approach to learning may consciously seek to use new learning strategies when called upon to deal with abstractions. A faculty member whose classroom is full of concrete, active learners may find it necessary to develop multiple examples for an abstract concept in order to help students understand. Both faculty and students can benefit from open discussion of such different approaches to learning and teaching.

Some research has used the MBTI to study personality profiles of accountants. The accounting firm of Ernst & Young reportedly has used Myers-Briggs for many years to develop profiles of their professional staff. A summary provided at a recent conference for accounting program administrators showed these results (Courtesy of Thomas J. Frecka):

17% ISTJ (Introversion, Sensing, Thinking, Judging)
17% ESTJ (Extraversion, Sensing, Thinking, Judging)
12% ENTJ (Extraversion, Intuitive, Thinking, Judging)
 9% INTJ (Introversion, Intuitive, Thinking, Judging)

Jacoby (1981) studied a sample of 333 accountants employed by public accounting firms in Washington, D.C. Jacoby found the following MBTI types in his sample:

19.8% ISTJ (Introversion, Sensing, Thinking, Judging)
13.8% ESTJ (Extraversion, Sensing, Thinking, Judging)
12.3% INTJ (Introversion, Intuitive, Thinking, Judging)

A follow-up study evaluating the perceptions of accountants by other professionals confirmed Jacoby's findings. According to these studies, it would appear that most accountants are perceived to be, as well as report themselves to be, likely to base judgments on impersonal analysis and logic (thinking), prefer a planned and orderly life (judging), are most comfortable dealing with known facts (sensing), and are usually more at ease when working with ideas than with people (introversion).

ASK A STUDENT

One way to explore different learning styles is to ask students how they learn. Try interviewing several different kinds of students (age, year in school, gender, race/ethnicity, etc.) to find out what helps them, what gets in their way, what excites them, etc. Some questions might be:

Tell me about a class where you really learned a lot. (Eliminate your own classes from their consideration.) Why do you think you learned so much? What part did other students play in your learning? What part did the instructor play? What about your own personal background? Did it contribute to your learning?

What kind of a learning environment is best for you? (You may need to add other questions to draw the student out, but the open-endedness of the question is meant to allow the student to include non-classroom experiences as well as the more traditional classroom environments.)

Were there particular classroom experiences that are or were helpful in your choice of a major or career? Why?

What is the purpose of college for you? Why do you think most students are here?

Adapted with permission from an assignment for the 1993 Great Lakes Colleges Association Design and Teaching Workshop by Jeannine Elliott.

Next to the core of personality research, the second circle of the learning style framework contains research on information-processing styles, that is, on how students absorb and use new information. One of the most prominent studies of this type is David Kolb's experiential learning model and the learning styles inventory (LSI) he developed to identify different ways of learning (Kolb, 1981). The experiential learning model essentially describes a circular pattern of learning experiences. Kolb maintains that for effective learning, the learner must experience the entire cycle. However, most people prefer one part of the cycle over other parts; their preference is their learning style, as identified by the LSI. Although some questions have been raised about the validity of the LSI instrument, the basic assumptions of the experiential learning model and Kolb's description of four approaches to learning have been useful to education researchers, including accounting educators.

Kolb's experiential learning model describes a four-step process. Learners most often begin with a concrete experience, which involves them in the topic or material in question. They then engage in reflective observations, considering the subject from several perspectives. This process leads to abstract conceptualization in which learners develop theories or generalizations about the topic. Finally, they use active experimentation to apply their theory to other, related material. Svinicki and Dixon (1987) applied Kolb's model to classroom activities. They suggested, for example, that concrete experience could include such activities as laboratories, observations, simulations, and field work; reflective observation could involve logs or journals, discussion, or brainstorming; abstract conceptualization could utilize lecture, papers, projects, and analogies; active experimentation could call for case studies, laboratories, simulations, and projects. Note that activities may be used in more than one way, depending on how the assignment is shaped. The goal is for students to experience all four parts of the learning cycle.

Svinicki and Dixon used the Kolb model to suggest sample instructional sequences for a number of disciplines. Building on their example, we suggest in Figure 3.4 a sample instructional sequence for an accounting topic. The sequence includes all four steps in Kolb's experiential learning cycle. Although an instructor could choose to start the sequence at any point, the entire cycle should be included to assure a complete learning experience.

Kolb's inventory of learning styles identifies four types or groups of learners based on their approach to knowledge. These different styles seem to draw individuals to specific careers or fields of study. The "divergers" prefer to approach learning through concrete experience and to process it through reflective observation; they are often humanities and liberal arts majors. The "accommodaters" also prefer to take in knowledge through concrete experience, but they like to process it through active experimentation; many business majors are in this group. The "assimilators" prefer to approach knowledge through abstract conceptualization and to process it through

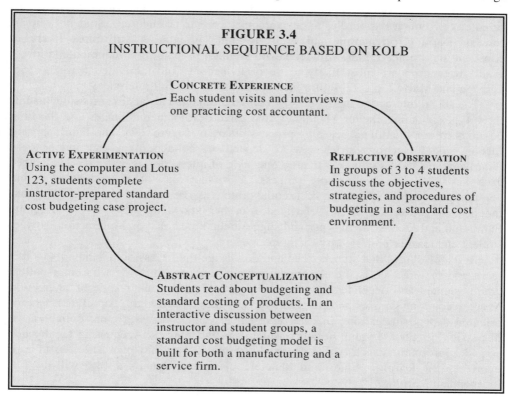

**FIGURE 3.4**
**INSTRUCTIONAL SEQUENCE BASED ON KOLB**

**CONCRETE EXPERIENCE**
Each student visits and interviews one practicing cost accountant.

**ACTIVE EXPERIMENTATION**
Using the computer and Lotus 123, students complete instructor-prepared standard cost budgeting case project.

**REFLECTIVE OBSERVATION**
In groups of 3 to 4 students discuss the objectives, strategies, and procedures of budgeting in a standard cost environment.

**ABSTRACT CONCEPTUALIZATION**
Students read about budgeting and standard costing of products. In an interactive discussion between instructor and student groups, a standard cost budgeting model is built for both a manufacturing and a service firm.

reflective observation; many of these students major in mathematics or the sciences. The "convergers" also approach knowledge abstractly but they prefer to process it through active experimentation; they are likely to major in nursing or engineering.

While most accounting classes will include all four types of students, research using different versions of the learning styles inventory suggests that many (but not a majority of) accounting majors are likely to be convergers or assimilators (Stout and Ruble, 1991). Strengths of the converger style include defining and solving problems, using deductive reasoning, and using practical application and conceptualization in making decisions. Strengths of the assimilator style include the ability to organize observations into an explanation or theory and the ability to develop plans to solve problems. Assimilators are less interested in practical applications. Note that both these styles use an abstract rather than concrete approach to learning.

Accounting faculty may use an understanding of learning styles to plan assignments, courses, and programs to include the entire cycle of learning experiences. In this way, every student will have an opportunity to use her preferred style of learning and also to practice and develop other styles. To be fully effective, a student's education should include the full cycle of learning experiences and the ability to use a variety of learning styles.

The third circle of the learning styles framework is research on social interaction, that is, on how students behave in the classroom, categorizing them, for example, as compliant, discouraged, independent, etc. Eison described students as learning-oriented (see courses as a way to encounter new ideas and increase knowledge), and grade-oriented (see courses as hurdles to be overcome, a test to be endured). Students who are low in learning orientation and high in grade orientation will most likely be conscientious "grade grinds." Students who are high in learning orientation and low in grade orientation are most likely to be or to become self-motivated learners. (See Claxton and Murrell, pp. 37-46, for brief descriptions and full references.)

The social interaction model developed by Fuhrmann and Jacobs sorts students into three types, echoing Baxter Magolda's first three developmental stages and the three columns in our intentional learning process diagram (Figure 2.2). The Fuhrmann and Jacobs model categorizes learners as dependent, collaborative, and independent. Fuhrmann and Jacobs point out that no one style of interaction is better than any other; each has a role in the learning process. A student may be dependent when just beginning to learn a subject or skill, collaborative as she develops understanding, and independent when she attains confidence in her knowledge. Figure 3.5 diagrams Fuhrmann and Jacobs' three types and suggests the kinds of social interaction between student and teacher preferred by each type.

Research shows that students can and do change their classroom behaviors as they learn and mature and as the classroom context changes. Students who enter college grade-oriented and dependent can be challenged to change their style of interaction. Many accounting courses and programs already move from highly structured, lecture-oriented dependent learning in early assignments and courses to more collaborative, discussion-oriented learning in later assignments and courses. Accounting faculty may consider information such as that depicted in Figure 3.5 as they plan activities to build upon student learning styles and generate classroom dynamics that will lead to independent learning.

```
╔═══════════════════════════════════════════════════════════════════╗
║                                                                     ║
║                           FIGURE 3.5                                ║
║            FUHRMANN-JACOBS MODEL OF LEARNERS AND TEACHERS           ║
║                                                                     ║
╚═══════════════════════════════════════════════════════════════════╝
```

| | Dependent | Collaborative | Independent |
|---|---|---|---|
| LEARNER'S STYLE | has little or no prior knowledge of subject | has some knowledge and ideas about subject | has skill or knowledge and confidence in ability |
| LEARNER NEEDS | structure<br>direction<br>encouragement<br>reinforcement | interaction<br>practice<br>observation<br>peer challenge<br>esteem | time<br>support<br>opportunity to experiment<br>resources |
| TEACHER ACTIONS | lecture<br>demonstrate<br>check<br>reinforce<br>encourage<br>test and grade | question<br>participate<br>model<br>coordinate<br>lead<br>grade | consult<br>listen<br>negotiate<br>facilitate<br>evaluate |

Based on Fuhrmann-Jacobs chart in Claxton and Murrell, p. 44.

The outermost circle of the learning styles framework is research on instructional preferences, that is, on teaching methods and the learning environment. This research confirms the intuition of many students that some courses or instructors are a better "fit" for them than some others. The Canfield Learning Style Inventory is one well-known instrument for assessing student instructional preference. This instrument results in measures on four dimensions: (1) conditions of learning which include affiliation with peers and instructor, structure, achievement of goals and independence, and attitude toward competition and authority; (2) content of learning which includes numerics, qualitative material, inanimate things or tasks, and people; (3) mode of learning which may be listening, reading, or direct experience; and (4) expectations of results in the form of a grade. There is also a Canfield Instructional Style Inventory that assesses the instructor's preferences on many of the same dimensions.

Research suggests that students are most comfortable and succeed best in courses that are compatible with their instructional preferences. Faculty have used the Canfield inventories to ascertain the learning preferences of their students and to initiate class discussion of learning styles and course assignments. In some cases, these discussions have led faculty to adjust teaching methods and coursework to include a variety of modes and conditions and have led students to understand and modify their own instructional preferences (Claxton and Murrell, 1987; Canfield, 1986).

Accounting faculty and students who might be uncomfortable talking specifically about learning to learn in an accounting class may find identification and discussion of learning and teaching styles a more fruitful approach to the same issues. After reviewing the learning style scores of students in a particular class, the instructor will know both students' preferences and their readiness for the materials and methods being used in the course. The instructor might then discuss these findings with the class and perhaps make adjustments or point out how certain assignments relate to specific student preferences or needs. The students in the class would gain insight into their own learning preferences in the context of a specific course. Motivated by their desire to succeed in the course, they might then consciously begin to learn to learn as they are learning accounting.

The studies of intellectual characteristics described in this section comprise only a sample of the resources available in this field. Much of it can be useful to faculty who want to add learning to learn to the accounting curriculum. Claxton and Murrell emphasize this aspect in the conclusion of their chapter on learning styles and college teaching: "....the issue of learning how to learn is underscored by the indication that students who learn about their own style achieve higher grades and have more positive attitudes about their studies, greater self-confidence, and more skill in applying their knowledge in college courses generally....And because teachers themselves find it helpful to know more about how their students learn and how to make needed changes in instruction, it may be that the long-term impact of learning style is the increase in achievement and self-confidence that comes about when faculty and students engage in an ongoing dialogue about how the student learns, how the teacher teaches, and how each can adapt to the other in the service of more effective learning" (p. 54). In other words, both students and faculty learn about learning by reflecting on their mutual experiences.

## 3.4 Motivation and Goals

In considering the characteristics of our students, we clearly have an interest in learning about their motivation and the goals they hope to achieve. For the purpose of this discussion, motivation is defined as a person's reason for doing something, in this case, a reason for learning. Educators commonly speak of motivation as extrinsic (from an external source) or intrinsic (from internal desire). Motivation may be a personal characteristic such as curiosity, a feature of the situation such as a teacher's enthusiasm, or a goal to be achieved such as a grade or a specific skill. In general, motivation is the result of a complex interaction between intrinsic and extrinsic influences and goals and the situation or setting in which action occurs.

In this section we summarize some current thinking about motivation, first in terms of what the student brings to the learning situation and then in terms of what happens in the course. Then we consider student and faculty goals as sources of motivation and as means to introduce learning to learn issues into the accounting classroom.

In addressing motivation, we acknowledge that learning is primarily the student's responsibility. Faculty can facilitate, but ultimately students must do the learning. In a recent monograph, Davis and Murrell (1993) reviewed the findings of four prominent researchers on student life: Astin, Pace, Tinto, and Pascarella. All four researchers agree that the most important factor in student success is involvement—with faculty, peers, and college life as well as with studies. Students who are integrated into the life of the campus will most likely be motivated to remain in school and meet their academic and career goals.

Most students bring both intrinsic and extrinsic motivation to their college work. Many will have been conditioned by previous educational experiences to respond more to external influences than to their own interests. They will have learned how to impress or please their teachers, how to pass exams with minimal effort, how to cobble together some sources into what they call a term paper. In doing so, they may have ignored subjects that would have interested or pleased themselves, neglected the broad picture in order to memorize details, failed to develop and express their own ideas in writing. They will have found a way to meet minimal course performance standards, without enjoying the opportunity to think or learn or entertain new ideas.

Educators have long known that extrinsic motivations are less effective than intrinsic reasons for learning. In a review of the research, McKeachie and others pointed out that, particularly at the beginning of a task, students motivated by external rewards tend to do more work but do it less well than students with internal motivation (McKeachie et al., 1986). This suggests that, especially in introductory courses, faculty interested in depth and quality over quantity of student work should emphasize intrinsic motivations. Research also shows that emphasis on extrinsic motivation may actually reduce intrinsic motivation for a task or learning. Thus, for example, an overemphasis on grading (10 points for this, 15 points for that, never do anything without getting points for it) may diminish a student's interest in exploring a topic beyond the bare requirements of the assignment.

Accounting students may be particularly vulnerable to an emphasis on extrinsic motivation. Some students take accounting for externally-oriented reasons: to gain entrance to or meet requirements for a business major; to satisfy a parent who is an accountant; to earn a credential that will look good on a future resume. These extrinsic motivations may be adequate to get students through a course, but they will not be sufficient to motivate students to learn to learn. Other students may enter accounting with more internally-oriented goals: to explore the field as a possible career; to understand the role of accounting in business; to develop skills they can use in a career or volunteer activities. These students are more ready to learn, but they can be easily discouraged if a course or program emphasizes external rewards and minimizes self-motivated learning.

Fortunately, most human beings possess several basic qualities that offer intrinsic motivation for learning. Faculty can build on these to encourage students to become conscious, independent learners. We will suggest three such qualities here: curiosity, self-esteem or a sense of competence, and the need for achievement, and will suggest how they relate to the attributes of intentional learning. First, most people enjoy learning and doing new things, particularly if those things are new enough to be challenging but not so new as to be totally alien. Students' curiosity will lead them to practice the attributes of questioning, organizing new knowledge, and connecting new knowledge with old. Second, a desire for self-esteem or competence will motivate a person to learn or develop new skills; an interest in competence may lead a student to reflect on learning and on how she is growing in knowledge. Third, the need for achievement motivates people to take action, particularly if there is a reasonable chance of success; this need may lead to the practice of adapting, of putting knowledge to new uses. While faculty cannot create or control student motivation, they can structure the learning situation to encourage the kinds of motivation that will lead to effective intentional learning.

Unfortunately, some characteristics of American education run counter to the goal of intentional learning. For example, students see education as the accumulation of class time and credits. They speak of the future as, "when my four years are up," as if they are in prison instead of in college. Faculty have described a student habit some call "bitting," that is, the collection of bits of information from notes or texts, just enough to pass a multiple-choice test (Richardson, 1986). A chemistry professor called this "nugget gathering," describing his senior students as "chipmunks or squirrels, storing away separate little chunks of knowledge" with no idea why or how or if they were related, but certain that "the more nuggets they gathered, the greater their chances of being accepted to medical school" (Schroeder, 1993). Encouraging intentional learning in such a setting will require thoughtful and persistent restructuring of the typical learning situation.

Students asked to analyze what kinds of classes have motivated them, commonly report eight characteristics as major elements in motivation (Davis, 1993, pp. 194-95):

Instructor's enthusiasm
Relevance of the material
Organization of the course
Appropriate difficulty level of the material
Active involvement of students
Variety
Rapport between teacher and students
Use of appropriate, concrete, and understandable examples

Most of these elements can be controlled or at least influenced by the instructor. Knowing and considering the abilities and interests of the students can help an instructor organize the course, select relevant and appropriate material, use examples and questions, and motivate students to prepare their assignments for class. Involvement, variety, and rapport empower students to take responsibility for learning that can go beyond the basic requirements of the course.

Two other motivational elements should be mentioned here: grades and the need for affiliation. The possibility of earning a good grade can be a positive incentive for many students, but the fear of failure is usually a disincentive. Grades should be de-emphasized and success should be possible for most students to be motivated to learn. For example, a biochemistry professor at Florida State uses a contract approach to decrease emphasis on grades and increase student effort and involvement. He guarantees at least a C grade to students who sign and follow a contract that requires class attendance, specific study practices, and faculty conferences after exams. The contract improves the quantity and quality of effort for most of the students in the class (Tobias, Dougherty, and Raphael, 1994).

Affiliation or the desire to be liked can work both for or against student motivation. A student who wishes to affiliate with the instructor or with the best students or with successful members of the profession will be motivated to learn. A student whose affiliation is toward peers who do not value learning will not be motivated to learn. Development of rapport in the class and emphasis on the importance of learning to the profession should help to increase the positive affiliations of students.

Both faculty and students are motivated by the goals they bring to a course. Faculty generally have several broad objectives, usually stated in the syllabus and sometimes dictated by the department's curriculum as a whole. Faculty may also have a number of more specific goals for a course, often left unstated. Some examples might be: "encourage students to major in accounting," "prepare students to succeed in business," "help students learn to learn." Students will bring their own goals, both extrinsic and intrinsic, to the same course. These goals may be as specific as "learn certain tax rules and regulations" or as general as "get acquainted with other students and have fun in class." Students are seldom asked to articulate their own course goals, but they will be motivated by them. The compatibility of course goals and student goals will very largely determine the amount of effort a student devotes to the course.

Under the auspices of the National Center for Research to Improve Postsecondary Teaching and Learning (NCRIPTAL), Stark and associates developed a series of Student Goals Exploration inventories designed to elicit course-level student goals. These adaptable instruments are available for institutional and classroom research, and for exploring student goals for their major. The instruments have been used at a number of institutions to assist with course and curriculum planning, to improve teaching and learning, to assist with recruitment and retention efforts. Faculty have found the classroom research model to be particularly useful in developing and discussing course goals (Stark et al., 1991).

Experience has shown that discussing course goals is a good way to encourage students to take responsibility for their own learning in the course. Faculty may use the

---

### STRATEGIES FOR MOTIVATING STUDENTS

1. Set high but realistic expectations for class.
2. Help students set achievable goals for themselves.
3. Tell students what they need to do to succed in your course—don't force them to guess.
4. Strengthen students' self-motivation by minimizing instructor power and extrinsic rewards.
5. Avoid creating intense competition among students.
6. Be enthusiastic about your subject.
7. Work from students' strengths and interests.
8. When possible, give students some choice on assignments or topics.
9. Increase the difficulty of material as the term progresses.
10. Vary your teaching methods.
11. Emphasize mastery rather than grades.
12. Design tests that encourage the kind of learning you want students to achieve.
13. Avoid using grades as threats.
14. Give students feedback as quickly as possible.
15. Reward success.

Based on Chapter 23, "Motivating Students," in Barbara Gross Davis, *Tools for Teaching,* 1993.

SGE inventory and discuss results with the class, or they may use selected portions of the instrument and add their own questions. Students may also be asked to add items to the list of potential course goals. The value of the exercise is not so much in the development of a long list as it is in the discussion of the goals. Faculty who find that student goals are not compatible with course goals may want to modify their own goals or else introduce assignments designed to help students change their goals. Students may decide they are in the wrong course or they may negotiate ways to add their own goals to course goals. In either case, discussion of goals will lead to clarity of purpose for both faculty and students.

Accounting faculty who want to include learning to learn in their accounting courses may find discussion of course goals helpful. The course goals will focus on accounting, but they may also include some goals related to the attributes of intentional learning. For example, course goals could include "encourage students to ask questions about their reading," or "students will learn to make connections between accounting practice and the success of a business." Asking students to articulate their goals for a course will force them to confront their own motivations and will stress their personal responsibility for meeting their goals.

The specific motivation and goals of accounting students require some further exploration. Students may be unpleasantly surprised when they confront the new realities and demands of the profession. They may resist changes in the curriculum that press them to develop communication and interpersonal skills and to learn to learn. They may have a very limited view of the profession and a very narrow vision of what their education should be.

There is, in fact, some evidence that students who make an early commitment to an accounting major have somewhat narrower goals for their education than do students who transfer to an accounting major. Inman, Wenzler, and Wickert (1989) reported the following differences in college goals of accounting majors, based on an analysis of 1986 graduates:

| Goal rated very important or essential | Transfer to Accounting | Always in Accounting |
|---|---|---|
| **COLLEGE GOALS** | | |
| Increase self-directed learning | 55% | 36% |
| Develop clear thinking ability | 81% | 65% |
| Develop creative capacities | 43% | 40% |
| **PERSONAL GOALS** | | |
| Influence social values | 29% | 27% |
| Be very well off financially | 58% | 79% |
| Help others in difficulty | 68% | 44% |

The sources of differences indicated here are not clear, but the findings suggest that the most well rounded accounting graduate may be one who started out undecided or majoring in something else. For this reason, accounting faculty should be particularly concerned about engaging students' interest in the introductory courses. The AECC's position statement on the first course in accounting offers a number of suggestions and stresses the need for creative changes in this course. Because the introductory course may be the only accounting course taken by non-majors, it is the profession's best opportunity to attract the kind of student who will become an intentional learning accountant.

It is discouraging to see that at the end of their programs, only two-thirds of graduates who were always accounting majors saw "Develop clear thinking ability" as an important college goal. It is even more discouraging to note that only 36% of these majors saw "Increase self-directed learning" as an important goal of their college education. Clearly this attitude presents a challenge for accounting educators to persuade students that learning to learn is an essential element in their preparation to become professional accountants.

# Chapter Four
# TEACHING AND THE PROCESS OF LEARNING

To help students learn, faculty need knowledge of the subject matter—its organization, methods of inquiry, principles and theories; knowledge of students—who they are and how they think; and knowledge of effective teaching strategies and skills. We assume that accounting professors know their subject. Knowledge about students and how this knowledge may be acquired has been discussed in Chapter Three. We turn here to knowledge about teaching and learning, and suggest how faculty can prepare their students to become lifelong, independent learners.

We assume that our readers have tried a number of the strategies and techniques we discuss here, but they may not always be sure why or how these strategies do or do not work. This chapter will offer a variety of choices that can lead to effective learning for accounting students. We do not claim that all of these choices will work for all faculty and all kinds of students, but we believe that most accounting faculty will find here some ideas they can adapt for use in their own classes.

We will address teaching and learning processes that can promote the attributes of intentional learning described in Chapter Two. This chapter includes the following sections: (1) the integration of learning to learn into the accounting curriculum as a whole; (2) planning a course to include learning to learn; (3) teaching strategies and roles that encourage the attributes of intentional learning; (4) the effect of the learning context or climate on the quality of learning; (5) the results and evaluation of successful student learning; (6) recommendations for teaching and learning.

## 4.1 Learning to Learn in the Curriculum

To introduce learning to learn into their program, faculty should consider the accounting curriculum as a whole, as well as how and what is taught in specific courses. We offer here some suggestions for incorporating learning to learn in the accounting curriculum.

In another context, Stark and others have defined curriculum as an academic plan. Eight elements to be considered as part of the plan are listed in Figure 4.1. Taken together, these elements are the building blocks of a coherent academic plan. To assure the integrity of the curriculum, each element should contribute to the overall objectives of the plan. Thus, for the new accounting curriculum, each element of the academic plan should promote the student's ability to learn. No one plan will be appropriate for all institutions or all accounting students. We suggest, however, that attention to the elements of the academic plan could be a good way to begin incorporating learning to learn into the accounting curriculum. For example, purpose could be defined as preparing future accountants who will be lifelong learners; content then would include both accounting knowledge and learning strategies. Each element of the curriculum plan could be developed in ways that specifically include learning to learn.

---

**FIGURE 4.1**
ELEMENTS OF THE ACADEMIC PLAN

1. PURPOSE - the knowledge, skills, and attitudes to be learned
2. CONTENT - the subject matter within which the learning experiences occur
3. SEQUENCE - an arrangement of the subject matter intended to lead to specific outcomes for learners
4. LEARNERS - information about the learners for whom the plan is desired
5. PROCESS - the instructional experiences that lead to learning
6. RESOURCES - the materials and settings to be used in the learning process
7. EVALUATION - the strategies used to determine if skills, knowledge, attitudes and behavior change as a result of the learning process
8. ADJUSTMENT - changes in the plan to increase learning, based on experience and evaluation

From Stark and associates, work in progress

---

Addressing content as an element of the academic plan raises a crucial question for accounting educators. What is or should be the knowledge base for future accountants? If faculty interpret content as all the current rules and standards of their field, they may find themselves "teaching" far more than students can effectively "learn." If, on the other hand, faculty consider content to be a set of basic accounting principles and the ability to find and apply accounting information, they will be able to combine both accounting knowledge and intentional learning attributes in their academic plans.

Sequence, another element of the plan, can apply to the curriculum as a whole and to individual courses. Some accounting programs are experimenting with the arrangement of courses and/or with the order of materials within courses. Brigham Young University, one of the AECC grant schools, has redesigned the junior year into a 24 credit accounting core that uses five business cycles to teach nine competencies. Courses are integrated and taught in 3-hour blocks, thus eliminating the boundaries between courses. Instead of teaching three 50-minute classes each week, a professor may have responsibility for a 3-week segment of four 3-hour classes per week. He will be dealing with a particular business cycle from the perspective of his discipline and expertise, demonstrating in how he teaches as well as what he teaches, the interrelationships of accounting principles and procedures. Faculty work together to sequence material and learning experiences within the integrated core. Of course, BYU faculty have modified other elements of curriculum as well.

Faculty interested in changing the accounting curriculum could begin with any element of the academic plan. But if change is to be successful, the elements of curriculum in the plan must be compatible. Changing one element will lead to changes in others. If the purpose is to prepare students to be independent learners, but the process is lecture courses and multiple choice exams, the purpose is unlikely to be fulfilled until the process and evaluative procedures are changed. Similarly, if the process is changed from lecture to discussion, group work, and case studies, the content will be modified in both subject and quantity. Attention to the elements of the academic plan and their relationships could provide a road map for coherent curricular change.

Faculty could approach curriculum change by focusing on the attributes of intentional learning as the purpose of the academic plan. Here we return to the intentional learning diagram discussed in Chapter Two, and add a new level, the teacher's role, to the scheme. The teacher's role changes as the learner becomes more independent. The teacher provides leadership and organization to help beginning learners attain knowledge and acquire learning strategies. As learners develop more sophisticated intellectual skills, the teacher's role becomes guiding and mentoring the learner's efforts. For advanced, independent learners who are practicing the attributes of intentional learning, the teacher becomes a mentor and colleague.

The changing nature of the teacher's role echoes the developmental process described by Baxter Magolda and the social interaction model of Fuhrmann and Jacobs (see Chapter Three). It seems clear that freshman and sophomore absolute knowers look to the authority of their teachers. The sophomore/junior transitional knowers expect faculty to help them understand and apply what they are learning. The advanced or employed independent and contextual knowers want faculty and supervisors who promote mutual exchange of ideas and who treat them as colleagues. The cumulative nature of the intentional learning process is seen in the increasing independence of these learners.

As discussed in Chapter Two, the intentional learning process is cyclical as well as cumulative. While students move systematically through the process to develop independence as learners, they may also circle back with increasing sophistication as they gain knowledge of their subject, and skill in using the learning attributes. Thus all the learning attributes could be introduced early in a student's program on a limited scale. The AECC's statement on the first course in accounting calls for teaching students to learn on their own at the very beginning of their programs. The intentional learning process suggests that the first course should focus on questioning and organizing, but might also introduce students to the other learning attributes.

The view of intentional learning as a cumulative process can be used to guide curriculum planning. As the following diagram suggests, the curriculum could systematically focus on the learning attributes in sequence. The first column in Figure 4.2 could be seen as the freshman-sophomore years or the introductory accounting course. Although the focus is on acquiring knowledge, attributes of intentional learning may also be practiced. The beginning learner will develop confidence in asking questions and in organizing knowledge into the patterns of the discipline. The teacher will lead the learner toward independent learning by gradually reducing teacher authority and increasing student responsibility. The second column could represent intermediate work at the sophomore-junior level, with focus on developing intellectual skills. Students at this point should be learning theory and solving problems; teachers at this level should guide students to consciously practice the attributes of questioning, organizing, and connecting. In the third column we see the learner who is able to use all the attributes of learning. These will be advanced students who are capable of researching and analyzing complex issues and of reaching creative solutions. They will also be self conscious learners who reflect on their learning experiences and adapt to

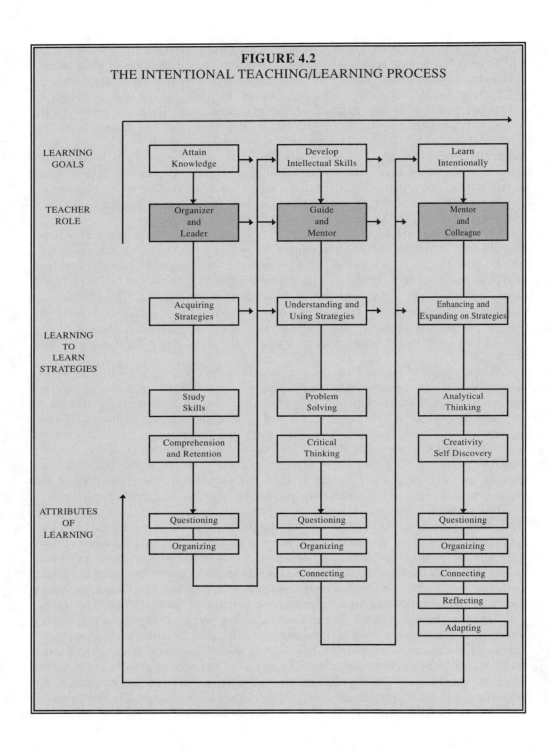

**FIGURE 4.2**
**THE INTENTIONAL TEACHING/LEARNING PROCESS**

new requirements. These learners will see their teachers as colleagues. As they approach each new course or topic, as students, or later as practitioners, they will consciously repeat the cycle of the intentional learning process but with increasingly sophisticated awareness and skill.

The approach depicted in the diagram has several implications for accounting educators. Looking at the curriculum as a whole, faculty might target specific courses or segments of the curriculum which would emphasize and require development of particular learning attributes. For example, faculty might review the introductory course to assure that it encourages questioning and organizing. One reason that students have difficulty learning and remembering the material in introductory courses is that they do not yet have an intellectual structure within which to organize new knowledge. The first course in accounting should help students ask good questions and organize their developing knowledge. Discussion of these goals could also help two-year and four-year college faculty review the articulation between their programs.

Students need to develop learning skills in logical order. Before they try handling complex case study analysis, they need experience with problem solving and critical thinking. Students also need encouragement and confidence to use their own intellectual abilities. This suggests that faculty should sequence both individual courses and the whole curriculum to increase student independence. Courses that offer opportunity to practice certain learning attributes might become at least informal prerequisites to others that require those abilities. The curriculum as a whole should move students toward intellectual independence and the development of all of the attributes of intentional learning.

As this discussion suggests, including learning to learn in the accounting curriculum requires more than just introducing a few new assignments or teaching techniques. The climate of the program will be different if students are consciously learning to learn as well as learning accounting principles. The roles of both students and faculty will change as students become independent learners and as faculty move from leading to guiding to mentoring students.

## 4.2 Planning a Course to Include Learning to Learn

Most college courses are planned by a single faculty member or, in a course with multiple sections, by a small faculty group. In planning a course, faculty are most strongly influenced by their academic discipline, their scholarly and pedagogical beliefs, and their understanding of the purpose of education. They will also be influenced by the local context, including textbooks, student characteristics, college and program mission and goals, and external constituencies such as accrediting bodies or professional associations (Stark et al., 1989).

In planning a course most faculty first consider the content to be covered. Then they may consider how it will be covered and what students will be doing in the course. We suggest careful attention to the process by which students will learn as well as to content. To facilitate course planning we suggest the following questions:

1. What do I want students to know at the end of this course?
2. What do I want students to be able to do at the end of this course?
3. What attributes of intentional learning will students develop in this course?

Many faculty "inherit" courses with departmentally mandated objectives or even a standard syllabus. Some courses are essentially "designed" by the choice of textbook, which may come with test banks, practice sets, teacher guides, lecture outlines, even overheads. Faculty teaching such courses may change textbooks or tinker with details of the syllabus, but they seldom have the opportunity to reconfigure the course as a whole. We suggest that the questions offered here, and particularly the attention to learning attributes, could be a starting point for revitalization of such courses.

When considering the learning process as part of the course plan and purpose, faculty need to be aware of factors that can discourage learning. Many circumstances in American higher education work against the attributes of learning that we are suggesting here. Some of these obstacles include class size, student preparation and readiness, college climate and expectations, and the size, shape, and furnishings of available classrooms. Faculty can work around many of these deterrents to assure that at least some of the learning attributes are included in each course. The curriculum should be planned and coordinated so that while acquiring content, the accounting student will also develop and use all of the attributes of intentional learning.

Several models exist for the course planning process. Some involve systematic use of faculty development staff, others encourage colleague consultation, either within or across departments. All these approaches to course design have in common attention to the content, the learner, teaching strategies, learning activities, and the course context. These can be addressed in any order, but all should be covered in the course plan. (For more on course design, see Stark and Lowther, 1986; Diamond, 1989; Lovell-Troy and Eickmann, 1992.)

To aid in planning a course to include learning to learn, we suggest using the matrix depicted in Figure 4.3. The matrix includes three aspects of a course which we will be discussing later in this chapter; we see these aspects as major influences on the development of the attributes of intentional learning. A course plan might consciously include attention to one or more of the attributes of intentional learning. While some courses might emphasize one attribute, the most advanced courses should call upon students to use all five attributes of intentional learning.

For example, to use the matrix to design a junior/senior level course in federal tax, an instructor would begin by drafting answers to our three questions about the course: What do I want students to know, to do, to develop as learners? The instructor might produce a list of 5 to 7 principles of taxation that students should know and technical skills that they should be able to demonstrate. The instructor would consider that these students have completed two or three years of college work, including at least one year of accounting principles. The students would probably have some ability to question and to organize knowledge, but would need help with the other learning attributes. Since tax would be a new aspect of accounting for them, the course should include ways to help them see where taxation fits in the knowledge structure of accounting. The instructor will want to help them connect knowledge about tax with their understanding of the objectives of financial reporting and also with their understanding of business, political processes, and historical events.

Using the matrix depicted here, the instructor will consider teaching strategies that encourage questioning, organizing, and connecting in our tax course. She will adjust the learning context, in so far as possible, to make students comfortable with the class and

**FIGURE 4.3**
CULTIVATING THE ATTRIBUTES OF LEARNING

Aspects of the Course

| Attributes | Teaching Strategies | Learning Context | Results and Evaluation |
|---|---|---|---|
| QUESTIONING | | | |
| ORGANIZING | | | |
| CONNECTING | | | |
| REFLECTING | | | |
| ADAPTING | | | |

with each other. She will articulate the results she hopes to achieve and devise means for evaluating them. For example, she might want the students to know enough about taxation so that they can recommend strategies to minimize taxes for a client. She might plan a variety of teaching strategies from introductory lectures about tax law to a case study that requires students to analyze a business's tax liabilities. She might plan a final project that evaluates the results of learning by asking students to study a set of facts and data and make recommendations to a hypothetical client that would minimize the client's taxes. Students in such a course could be expected to ask questions, organize knowledge, and make connections as they learn about taxation. They would reflect on their learning and adapt it to new circumstances in the final, evaluative project.

To prepare students to succeed in such a course, the instructor needs a syllabus that sets out her goals and the processes she will use to reach them. Students accustomed to passive learning may resent being required to involve themselves in analysis, discussion, and group projects with the teacher as a guide instead of a leader and organizer. Students need to understand the reasons for their own discomfort and for the teaching/learning strategies used in the course. A discussion of course goals as suggested in Chapter Three could be helpful. Faculty who expect students to develop learning attributes need to include these attributes in the course goals and help students understand the relationship between the attributes and the teacher's role, teaching strategies, and learning activities of the course.

The sections that follow in this chapter will suggest how aspects of the course might encourage the attributes of learning. These aspects—teaching role or strategies, the learning context, and course results and evaluation—can all be planned to emphasize any one or all of the learning attributes. Faculty who want to include attributes of learning in an accounting course should plan specifically how each course aspect will enhance the desired attributes.

### 4.3 Teaching Roles and Strategies for Learning

A good teacher will be a learner as well, learning about her discipline, students, learning theory and new teaching roles and strategies. Resources are available to offer fresh insight on these matters to even the most experienced and able college teachers. Research shows that using a variety of teaching strategies to engage students in learning enhances both learning and motivation. Faculty who review this research find that learning theory and the experience of others can be helpful as they shape curriculum and courses to include new emphasis on learning to learn.

In considering the teacher's role in helping students learn to learn, it is useful to think of the ultimate role of the teacher as a mentor or coach of learning rather than a professor of knowledge. Of course this approach is not new, but it fits well our desire to focus on learning rather than teaching. The coach or mentor is a colleague who helps individuals enhance their professional performance. Faculty who see themselves as mentors will concentrate on enhancing the performance of the learners in their classroom, rather than on their own performance. Schon's reflective practicum (see Chapter One) is a good example of teaching as coaching or mentoring.

We now present a series of common teaching roles and strategies and show how they can enhance the attributes of intentional learning. Within the limitations of a short monograph, we could not cover all the possible roles and strategies that could encourage learning. References in our resources list will lead readers to some of the literature in this field. Our choice is to present a limited number of teaching strategies in enough detail so a reader can use these ideas without turning to additional materials. In this discussion we follow a rough progression from the most structured and least interactive strategies to the least structured and most interactive approaches, from the most teacher-dominated to the most student responsibility. This order also echoes the learning process diagram presented in Figure 4.2 and the development of intentional learning attributes. The teaching strategies presented here can all be adapted by individual accounting instructors to their courses and to the particular needs of their students. The goal is to empower students to take responsibility for their learning so they can become independent learners.

### 4.3.1 Lecture

The teaching strategy most commonly used in higher education is the formal lecture. This is true in spite of the availability of many other strategies and research showing that lecturing is not the most effective way to help students learn. It is widely assumed that lecturing is about the only strategy available to teach large classes (100 or more students) and that most students prefer discussion classes. In fact, lectures are used in small classes as well as large, and some students prefer lectures, partly because little energy and little preparation is required of them. Lectures can be designed to include student involvement and can be an effective strategy for achieving some learning goals. We therefore suggest here some reasons to use lecture and some strategies for involving students actively in the lecture/learning process.

Brookfield (1990) suggests five reasons for choosing to lecture: (1) to establish the broad outlines of a body of material, (2) to set guidelines for independent study, (3) to model intellectual attributes for students, (4) to encourage learners' interest in a topic,

(5) to set the moral culture for discussions. McKeachie's review of the research on lecturing shows that for simply conveying knowledge, lecture is as efficient as any other approach. But for other kinds of learning goals, such as long-term retention of material, problem solving, critical thinking, and motivation for lifelong learning, discussion type methods are more effective (McKeachie et al., 1986). To help students learn to learn, we need to decrease emphasis on lecture as a teaching strategy, and we need to modify how we use lectures.

A successful lecturer will model in the classroom the kind of energy, enthusiasm, and passion for learning she hopes to engender in students. The lecturer will, of course, be knowledgeable and well prepared. The lecture and the course will be well organized. The lecturer should also be willing to be revealed as human, through humor, personal references, an openness to new ideas. In lecturing, the instructor's role is to model the attitudes and learning attributes desired for students in the course. Thus, for example, the lecturer will raise questions and point out the role of questioning in learning to learn, or she will outline relationships between concepts to show students how knowledge can be organized, or she will bring in examples to connect the lecture topic to business problems or news events. The successful lecturer will be as interested in students as in the subject, aware of student interests and questions and willing to adjust the lecture to meet student needs.

It is possible to introduce learning experiences that lead students to develop questioning and organizing skills into even a very large lecture course. Research shows that students can concentrate on a lecture for fifteen or twenty minutes and then attention begins to wander. A lecturer might plan for this by stopping after twenty minutes to engage students in some kind of activity, as individuals, in pairs or small groups, or as a whole class. There are many ways to do this; we will mention only a few here. (See Frederick, 1986 for additional ideas.)

- The professor might pause to let students catch up with their notes and compare notes with a neighbor. Students could then raise questions about points of confusion which the professor could clear up before going on with the lecture.
- Students could divide into pairs or triads to discuss a problem or question arising from the lecture. After 8-10 minutes some groups might report, with others agreeing or disagreeing by show of hands. Then the professor could bring closure by summarizing the points raised or discussing the solutions proposed.
- At the beginning, middle, or end of a lecture, students could be asked to write a brief (one sentence? one page?) question about the topic, or summary statement of the lecture's main point, or example of the theory under discussion, or answer to a question about the lecture. These papers need not be graded, or even signed, but reading them will give the lecturer insight into the students' needs and some material to address in future classes.

### 4.3.2 Reading

Research suggests that many (but not all) students learn more from reading than from listening to lectures. When reading, they can go back over difficult material or, if one book does not communicate effectively, they can choose another. Unfortunately, however, some college students today do not read well or have not developed the habit of reading to gain information. Many, especially at the beginning of their college work, are not capable of reading critically, that is, of identifying faulty assumptions, comparing disparate viewpoints, analyzing a reading to determine the validity of its argument. Accounting faculty should be aware of resources (reading labs, tutors) available on campus to help students improve reading skills. Faculty can also guide students' reading by pointing out key ideas, providing study questions, or critiquing a reading with the class.

Faculty who want to emphasize learning to learn will need to go beyond the standard textbook in their reading assignments. Reference books, legal documents, business reports, professional accounting and business publications are possible sources for supplementary readings. Most textbooks will provide the basic information needed on the main topics of the course. To go beyond basic information, faculty may choose readings that raise questions, present problems, serve as examples, or engage students' curiosity or enthusiasm about the topic.

Carefully chosen readings can help students develop the attributes of intentional learning. For example, to help students practice asking questions about what they are reading, faculty could provide a set of questions to be applied to the reading of business editorials (What is the thesis? What are the assumptions behind the thesis?....support for the thesis? What questions are left unanswered?) Students could practice organizing the information in their course reading by making outlines, diagrams, or concept maps and then comparing their work with classmates. The teacher's role in selecting a variety of readings is to provide examples that help students make connections between new information and previous knowledge and experience.

A number of strategies can help engage students with their reading and promote intentional learning. Study questions can help students read carefully and with understanding. To be most effective, these questions should deal with issues and principles rather than focus on facts, figures, and terminology; written responses should be collected, discussed in class and any confusions cleared up. Students may be asked to keep a reading log in which they react to, reflect on, raise questions about, and organize details from their reading. Students may also be encouraged to work in study groups to review and discuss their reading and share questions and comments. Most students expect to do a significant amount of reading for most college courses. Using the strategies suggested here, reading can help students learn the attributes of intentional learning as well as the facts and theories of the course.

### 4.3.3 Discussion

It is widely recognized that involving students in discussion helps them develop sophisticated intellectual abilities. We can expect, then, that discussions will lead students to practice the attributes of intentional learning. Obviously, a discussion will involve students in asking and being asked questions. Discussion may also call upon students to practice organizing ideas and concepts into a logical structure, or it may reveal a student's faulty organization of material. Discussion of examples and experience can help students make a variety of connections between what they know, what they hear, what they and others say. Ideally, a good discussion includes opportunities to reflect on what is happening. Questions can help encourage reflection on the ideas generated in a discussion. Students engaged in discussion of case studies, open-ended problems, and broad issues will also find themselves adapting what they have already learned to help them address the issues raised in these kinds of discussions. While discussion is not the only way to encourage intentional learning, nor is it always the best way, it does provide a variety of opportunities for students to practice effective learning.

An instructor may choose discussion as a teaching strategy to achieve a number of different purposes. For example, a good discussion could spark student interest in a topic and motivate further learning. It could encourage commitment to an idea or action. Discussion can be used to reveal and examine student assumptions and to help students see a variety of perspectives on an issue or problem. In addition, a good discussion class can help students learn to listen closely, to understand and react to different ideas, and to express and support their own positions. Listening, understanding and communicating are important skills for learning to learn and for accountants to deal with clients and management.

In order to enjoy and benefit from a good discussion, both faculty and students need to be prepared. First, they need to be prepared on the topic to be discussed. This means the instructor knows what she wants to accomplish, chooses a topic suitable for class participation, and prepares several questions, stories, problems, and other techniques to generate discussion. Students must think about the topic in advance and do the reading, problems and research assigned for the discussion. Second, being prepared also means that both faculty and students think about and develop the skills of discussion learning. For faculty this means changing roles, giving up some control of class time and direction, risking some confusion and limited "coverage" of a topic, learning to step back and encourage students to talk to each other instead of to the teacher. For students, discussion requires learning to listen to peers as well as to the instructor, judging when to speak up and when to let others speak, adjusting to ambiguity and a variety of perspectives instead of listening to only one authoritative voice. Done well, a good discussion requires as much preparation as a brilliant lecture, but changes the teacher's role to participant instead of leader.

## ENCOURAGING DISCUSSION

If one or two students seem to dominate discussion and others are too shy to participate, you might limit students to two or three comments per class. This opens opportunity for the usually silent student. You might ask everyone to jot down a response to a question and then call on several students. Or you might try using a full moment of silence between asking a question and calling on students to answer. Faculty who have used this technique find that previously quiet students, given time to think, volunteer good comments. Both faculty and students will be uncomfortable with silence at first, so try this several times to give the practice a chance to work for you. For other suggestions on generating good discussions, see Frederick (1981), "The Dreaded Discussion."

In preparing for discussion, it is tempting to focus on content more than on process. This would be a mistake. The process is crucial to a successful discussion. The instructor may want to lead the class to a certain conclusion or raise a certain number of key points. Some guidance is essential, but too much will produce an artificial situation. A good discussion stays within the boundaries of relevance but pushes those limits and explores fresh territory. Faculty as well as students may expect new insights into the topic when discussion is allowed to flow freely. On the other hand, if questions are contrived or too limited, the class ends up as a question and answer session, almost an oral quiz. Students will be trying to guess what the instructor wants to hear rather than thinking about an issue or expressing their solutions to a problem. This experience can be frustrating for both faculty and students.

Preparation that focuses on process as well as content will include conscious decisions about how to encourage participation, what kinds of questions to ask, how to make best use of the setting, whether and how to grade students on discussion. One way to encourage broad participation is to engage the class in setting ground rules for discussion (for example, how many times, how often, how long an individual should speak). If the class agrees to these in advance, peer pressure will help control the overeager student who wants to turn discussion into a dialog between himself and the instructor. Shy students may be encouraged to participate by being asked to observe and report on the process, or periodically to frame the consensus they are hearing, or to write a summary or questions for the next session. Discussion questions should be open ended so that many possible answers could be right (for example, what options does the accountant for XYZ company have in handling inventory? or how would you use the information on the balance sheet to decide whether to accept this company as an audit client?).

The setting may help or hinder discussion and thus the opportunity to learn to learn. Ideally, a discussion class involves 12-20 students in a conference-type room, but most accounting classes are not that fortunate. If the chairs are not bolted to the floor, they should be arranged so that students can see each other, as well as the instructor. Even in a large lecture room, students can be encouraged to turn and look at their peers instead of always facing forward. Evaluating classroom participation can be difficult, and some professors philosophically oppose it, but students may expect it if discussion is important to the class. The evaluation should go beyond an impressionistic sense of who talks the most to include some acknowledgement of the quality of talk and the possibility of less vocal contributions. Faculty may find it helpful to make notes on student participation after each discussion class; faculty may also consider student self-evaluation and peer evaluation of contributions to discussion. Sharing responsibility for evaluating participation should emphasize student responsibility for learning through discussion.

Discussions should be planned to help students practice the attributes of intentional learning. For example, students can be given sample questions which can be applied to a number of different topics for small group or whole class discussions. A similar approach is the developmental discussion which requires students to go through four steps in discussing any topic: (1) formulate the problem, (2) suggest hypotheses, (3) gather relevant data, (4) evaluate alternative solutions. [For more on the developmental discussion, see McKeachie, 1994, p. 33-34.] The structured discussion helps students

---

### SOME SAMPLE DISCUSSION QUESTIONS

What problems do you see in . . . ?
What assumptions underlie . . . ?
What evidence supports your opinion about . . . ?
How does this concept/situation/proposal fit what you already know about . . . ?
What questions must be asked in order to . . . ?
What are the connections between . . . ?
In a different situation or context, how might you apply . . . ?

---

learn to address problems critically and systematically. The open discussion involves students in leading as well as participating in class. Discussions like these will be effective strategies for engaging students in the activities of intentional learning.

### 4.3.4  Group Learning

Another way to engage students in learning is to get them to work together. A group learning experience can be distinguished from discussion by its more structured nature and results. Generally a group will be given quite explicit instructions and will be expected to produce something — a solution to a problem, a project or report, a presentation on a specific topic. In group learning, the teacher's role becomes planner, facilitator, and occasionally participant. There are many terms for group learning: peer teaching, cooperative learning, and collaborative learning are some of these. All deemphasize competition and require that students take responsibility for group results as well as their own learning. Successful group learning requires that both faculty and students reject individualism in favor of a team approach. While this may be difficult, it is useful preparation for future accountants.

A helpful introduction to group learning is Johnson, Johnson, and Smith, *Cooperative Learning: Increasing College Faculty Instructional Productivity* (1991). The authors stress the importance of planning and preparation for effective group learning. Good results are not achieved automatically just by forming groups and assigning tasks. Specifically, there are five elements essential to effective cooperative learning: (1) positive interdependence (students sink or swim together), (2) face-to-face promotive interaction, (3) individual accountability, (4) social skills (such as leadership, trust, communication, conflict management), and (5) group processing (reflecting on the group experience and how it could be improved). Johnson, Johnson, and Smith offer specific suggestions for incorporating these elements into group learning activities.

Student groups may be formed for a number of different purposes. Students may be asked to discuss key points of reading or lectures in order to reinforce their understanding of facts and principles. A group may be formed to apply new knowledge to solving problems or to analyzing case studies. Groups may research topics or key questions and prepare a report or present two or three possible solutions to an issue. Some groups may be formed as mutual study support, in which students encourage and motivate one another to work through the material of the course or program. Group learning may be used to reinforce any aspect of the learning process.

For purposes of discussion here, we will divide group learning into three types: learning in pairs, learning in informal groups, learning in formal groups. All three types could serve a variety of purposes and all can be useful in even very large accounting classes.

Learning in pairs is perhaps the easiest type of group learning for both faculty and students to manage. At its simplest, this approach means asking each student to turn to another person and ask a question or discuss a topic. The groups can be easily varied (find a new partner and ask a different question), and most kinds of group assignments can be handled by two people. Working in pairs has a long history of success, in such settings as lab instruction and shared computer terminals.

---

### THE LEARNING CELL

Marcel Goldschmid of the Switzerland Federal Institute of Technology formalized the process of learning in pairs as the "learning cell." In this process, students first study an assignment and write questions about it. In class they divide into pairs and student A asks student B a question. After B answers (and is perhaps corrected and instructed by A), then B asks A a question. The process repeats as long as appropriate while the instructor circulates, asks or answers questions, and oversees the process. Another use of the learning cell would have each student study a different topic and then teach it to his partner.

Described in McKeachie, *Teaching Tips*, 1994

---

Learning in pairs could be useful to accounting students at any level. Students in the beginning course could quiz each other on the principles and theories they are learning, and bring their most difficult questions to the instructor for clarification (some faculty ask that questions be submitted on cards). Or they could share answers to assigned problems and talk about how they reached their solutions. Students in more advanced classes could teach each other certain tax laws or share analysis of a case study. Student A could propose a change in accounting practice for the company in the case and Student B would then be asked to analyze the effect on the company's profitability and risk. Students at this stage will be practicing reflecting and adapting abilities. Any number of topics and problems can be adapted to learning in pairs at any point in the accounting curriculum.

Learning in informal groups extends the concept of group learning. Informal groups are those formed on an ad hoc basis for a relatively short-term assignment (one class, one project, one week). The group need not be formally structured; three-four-five students sitting near one another could form a convenient group. They could be asked to do many of the kinds of things a pair of students might do, although obviously the larger the group the more structure is needed and the greater the possibility that someone might be left out of the interaction. It might be best to start a term with pairs and then move to groups of three or four as students learn to work together.

Introducing informal groups is a relatively low risk way to involve students in group learning. The project or assignment can be short and probably will not be formally graded. The time commitment can be limited and need not all be class time. Assignments should be very specific, well structured, and clear in purpose. Some examples of informal group projects might be: Answer specific questions about a company's balance sheet and share your group's answers with the class; Using a structured interview protocol provided by the instructor, interview a local business manager about his company's accounting practices; Read, discuss, and jointly prepare a critique of a journal article; Follow a business news story and report to the class on the story and how it is handled in the media.

Learning in formal groups requires carefully structured, long-term groups and projects. These groups might include 5-7 students, probably assigned by the instructor with some attention to a mix of talents, interests, and perspective. They will probably need to meet outside of class. Generally these groups will be graded, as a group and perhaps also individually. They may be expected to reflect on group process and critique one anothers' participation, as well as to produce a report or presentation or solution to a problem.

Formal group learning is probably best suited to advanced students who have had enough experience in groups to be comfortable with commitment to a formal group project. Faculty might assign them to groups based on their strengths and interests. Students might also self select by interest in an industry (health care, hospitality, automobiles), or in a career path (finance or tax oriented projects or problems). Some examples of formal group learning projects are:

- At Brigham Young University, students in the new accounting core work in formal groups of five to complete several assignments during each 7 week block, some in class, some outside. Groups change every 7 weeks, so that students can work with a variety of people. The first 3 groupings are assigned, the first to attain a mix of gender, ability, etc., others randomly. For the last block students select their own groups. Assignments may include projects, presentations of cases or problems, sometimes even taking a quiz together. Both faculty and students have been pleased with the group experience.

- At the University of Southern California, an accounting professor has a group of students actually run a business, for example, a local pizza franchise, or the college bookstore, for a day.

- In the AECC curriculum project at the University of Illinois/Notre Dame, students in the first accounting course work in groups of four as promoters of a hypothetical rock concert. Their job is to make a deal with the arena manager (the course instructor) to put on a concert. To do this they need to come up with numbers and contract terms that make sense to both parties. This involves the student groups in developing and using accounting information in a business decision situation.

- Arizona State University uses cooperative learning in its Accounting 230/240 (Uses of Accounting Information) course. Students meet in one 350-member megasection and two 44-member "breakout" sections each week. During the breakout sections, students work in groups on assignments such as a structured controversy debate on historical cost versus current cost as a generally accepted accounting practice, or an analysis of a company's financial statements from the perspective of a potential investor. Teaching assistants who lead the breakout sections get thorough preparation in the skills of facilitating group learning. Their training includes a three-day pre-semester workshop, weekly meetings together to preview class activities, and periodic meetings with senior faculty.

- At the University of Alabama, students in Financial Accounting I are randomly assigned to semester-long groups that are involved in two types of activities: (1) accounting, financial, and operating analyses of two sample companies' annual reports, (2) analysis and preparation of cases. These activities are designed to develop group analytical and decision-making skills.

As every teacher knows, the best way to learn anything is to teach it to someone else. Group work often involves "peer teaching" which encourages students to practice many of the attributes of intentional learning. They will be forced to ask questions, and answer them; they will have to organize their knowledge in meaningful ways; they will need to make connections with their own and another's previous knowledge. They can also be asked to reflect on their experience as teachers and learners and they may also then adapt that experience to other learning tasks. [For more on peer teaching, see Whitman, 1988.]

Some students and faculty object to group learning. Some students say they want to listen to the professor, not to their peers. Some faculty fear that group learning will be inefficient and confusing. Groups can't cover as much material in working together as a professor can in lecturing. These are serious concerns. They can be mitigated by carefully structuring the group work for maximum effectiveness. Group learning will not cover as much material as lecturing, but it will have compensating benefits. When successful, students actively engaged in group learning will be practicing the attributes of questioning, organizing, and connecting knowledge. They will be learning to work in teams, to communicate clearly and to listen to others. They will be learning to learn and to teach others, and they will be developing interpersonal skills they will need for successful careers in accounting. Finally, their learning is likely to be remembered longer and reinforced by their group interactions.

### 4.3.5 Problems, Practice Sets, and Case Studies

Problems, practice sets, and case studies are related activities that involve students in finding solutions, either as individuals or in groups. Problems are relatively limited exercises with clear-cut answers; practice sets generally involve a series of questions or activities about related data and may require students to make their own connections; case studies are more elaborate and ambiguous problems with no clear-cut solutions. These are all used in accounting education today and all have a role in developing the student's ability to learn. Learning to solve problems prepares the student to handle practice sets which in turn develop the student's ability to deal with the complexity of case studies. In terms of the learning diagram in Figure 4.2, the teaching process becomes more complex as the student moves from attaining knowledge to developing intellectual skills to intentional learning.

Problem-solving exercises should involve students in a series of activities that help them learn how to approach problems in general as well as how to solve a specific problem. The process should include at least these basic steps:

1. Defining the problem as clearly as possible, seeing its limits and its implications.
2. Assembling and evaluating all available relevant data, using research and analysis skills.
3. Identifying assumptions inherent in the problem and data and in their own approach to the task.
4. Examining potential solutions and their possible consequences, looking at a variety of options.
5. Adopting and evaluating a solution, considering its potential effectiveness.

All accounting students know that they will be doing problems as part of their coursework. Practically every chapter of every textbook includes problems that illustrate or apply the material presented in the chapter. Problems may also appear on exams. Students may perceive the problems as busywork, and give them only cursory attention. But well planned problem assignments can help students understand and retain the principles of the field and begin to enjoy the challenges of their future profession.

Beginning students are likely to focus more on whether they got the right answer than on how they reached the solution and what they are learning in the process. Yet, as most faculty know, students may learn more from analyzing and understanding their mistakes than from getting the answer right the first time. It is not easy to encourage students to examine and learn from their mistakes. To do so, we need to minimize the student's risk, perhaps by working in pairs and groups. Students can be encouraged to compare answers and, more important, compare how they reached them. They may solve problems in groups, working through each step together so that all see how to reach the answer as well as what the answer should be. Some programs are using computer software that records students' thinking processes as they solve problems so professors can see where difficulties lie.

Using problems to help students learn requires that they focus more on the process than on the solution. Students can be encouraged to ask questions like <u>how</u> and <u>why</u> and <u>when</u> might the process be different. They can be asked to connect a problem with a local, real life situation, or even to write their own problems for a fellow student to work. Working problems can help students learn to learn if the problems engage students more with meaning than with mechanics.

The practice set method of instruction may be used to assist students in organizing and connecting knowledge, and in learning to think analytically. Practice sets are offered by most accounting textbook publishers. Many are available as computer assignments. A focus on intentional learning does not require that instructors discard practice sets, but rather that they use them in new and purposeful ways. If properly constructed and administered, the practice set method of instruction can be an effective way to enhance the life-long learning skills of accounting students.

Practice sets in accounting courses can be used to encourage and motivate students to question accounting procedures and systems, to organize their knowledge as well as their effort, to connect and adapt learned theory and procedure, to reflect on the environment, setting, and context of the business simulation, and to adapt business solutions to the practice set requirements. Faculty can help students become intentional learners by discussing with them the learning and problem solving processes they are experiencing.

Perhaps the greatest danger in using practice sets is creating the impression that there are exact answers or solutions, and that, unless one discovers these, one will not be successful as an accountant. The practice set experience should develop an understanding of accounting procedure, theory, and issues; the attributes of intentional learning; and an appreciation of the complexities of accounting practice.

The case method has gained popularity as a way to teach students to think analytically and learn to make good decisions. Case studies are now available as computer simulations of business problems. More will be said about these in our discussion of technology. Many accounting professors are, of course, familiar with the case method which medical and law schools have used for many years. The case method is not yet widely used in undergraduate education, and we are still learning how and when to use it effectively. Many accounting faculty are finding the case method to be a promising way to enhance the learning of their more advanced undergraduate students. (Christensen, 1987; Knechel, 1992)

Essentially, a case is a story with characters, a plot, and a problem situation. A case may be a short paragraph or page simply describing a problem and the two or three people involved in it. Or the case may be long and complex, focusing on an entire business with many details, multiple problems, and a large cast of characters. Discussion of a case may be relatively structured, with the instructor asking a carefully designed set of questions that lead students to examine all the nuances of the case. Or discussion may be completely open, with students expected to do the analysis and lead the class themselves. Obviously, students who are inexperienced with the case method should begin with relatively simple cases and the instructor should provide patterns for analysis and structured discussion. More advanced students may progress with experience to more complex cases and less structured assignments.

A case method course or assignment requires strong commitment from both students and faculty. To be successful, the students need to have basic knowledge of the subject, the motivation to work intensively alone and with other students, and enough maturity to risk sharing their ideas in the classroom. Faculty, in addition to firm control

---

### FORMAT FOR CASE PRESENTATIONS

1. Present a concise statement of the accounting issue(s) involved in the case.
2. Examine the economic substance of the transaction that created the accounting issue(s) under consideration in the case.
3. Based on your work in 1 and 2, provide a discussion of alternative solutions to (i.e., resolutions of) the accounting issue(s) identified in the case.
4. Present your recommendation of what, in your professional judgment, is the most appropriate solution to the accounting issue(s) identified in the case.

Used in Financial Accounting 310 at the University of Alabama by Professors Tom Lee, Mike Dugan and Mary Stone

of the subject, need skill in and understanding of the case method. Their role is to assign cases, guide student analysis, and participate more as coach and colleague than as professor. Faculty need to be able to listen, to question, to guide discussion without forcing its direction. The temptation to "take over" the discussion must be steadfastly resisted. Like students, faculty need to be willing to take risks in the case method classroom. Both faculty and students may need to learn new roles if they are to be successful in using case method study to develop intentional learning.

Advantages of the case method include: students learn to analyze real-life situations; they learn to make decisions based on analysis; they are involved in the learning process; they learn to express and practice communicating their ideas in a group; they learn to see and decide among a variety of responses to a given situation. In a successful case method course, the class may develop a sense of community, learning to function as a cohesive learning group. All of the students will be heavily involved in preparing cases, in presenting their own analyses of and solutions to the case problem, and in listening to and critiquing the ideas of their peers. Principles and theories will evolve through open discussion that may bring new ideas to the instructor as well as to the students.

All five attributes of intentional learning can be called upon in a case discussion course. The learner can practice questioning in preparing the case and in class discussion. Organizing ideas will be an essential part of case preparation and will lead to connecting knowledge from case discussion with other cases and with work experience. Reflecting will occur as the case discussion is debriefed in class and as the learner uses what is learned from one case to prepare for discussion of another case. And finally, adapting is what case method teaching is all about, applying what has already been learned to new situations as presented in the cases assigned in the class.

### 4.3.6 Writing

Effective communication skills are highly prized in the accounting profession. While oral communication skills are also important, we will focus here on developing writing skills. Freshman writing classes do not usually prepare students to handle the demands of writing in business careers. Many business schools offer or require an additional course in business or technical writing, taught by English Department faculty, using assignments geared to business topics. Attention is paid to audience and purpose as well as to content and clarity and the conventions of sentence structure and punctuation. Another and potentially more productive arrangement is teamwork between a business instructor and an English instructor or a "writing across the curriculum" coordinator who serves as guide.

If accounting students are to take writing seriously as part of their professional preparation, they need to write often and well in all of their accounting courses. Even in large courses, students should be asked to write brief exercises or short essay answers on quizzes. In smaller classes, students may be asked to write memos, letters to clients, short reports. Advanced students in seminars might be writing research reports for presentation to the class, or preparing thorough analyses of case studies.

The experience of writing can help students both learn the content of the course and reflect on how they are learning it. We will address these two goals separately, but many assignments could well achieve both. For example, an essay exam question could require students to apply specific knowledge from the course and also to demonstrate their ability to organize and reflect on that knowledge. In any case, writing in accounting courses should focus on learning and on accounting, not on writing for its own sake.

A number of writing tasks can help students develop the attributes of intentional learning. For example, students can be asked to write questions about what they are studying, or they can be asked to organize new knowledge into outlines and diagrams or they can be asked to write a paragraph connecting a current business event with a theory they are learning in class. The one-minute paper idea can be used even in a large lecture class to ask students to take one minute to reflect on what has been said and to write about the key idea presented, a question still unanswered, or a remaining point of confusion. A longer exercise of writing for five minutes on a specified topic without stopping—called a focused free writing—can help students clarify and organize their thoughts. Faculty reading these brief papers will get a good idea of what their students are learning and what they still need to know. Students will practice expressing what they know and asking what they don't know. The brief written exercises can be shared in pairs or small groups to increase student awareness of learning attributes.

Keeping a journal is another excellent way for students to practice writing and to reflect on their learning. Journal assignments need to be made explicit, so students don't fall into the trap of writing a diary. For example, students could be asked to interview practicing accountants and describe their career experiences, or to follow a current business controversy in the *Wall Street Journal* and discuss the accounting issues involved. They may also be asked to write specifically about their learning experience in the course. Faculty should set guidelines for content and should collect, read, and comment on the journals periodically. Some faculty grade journals, some do not. Our recommendation is to grade them, perhaps on a satisfactory/unsatisfactory basis, and to make the grading criteria clear at the beginning.

Journals are excellent opportunities for students to practice the attributes of intentional learning. They may raise questions about issues that puzzle them, or practice creating order out of the chaos of new learnings. They may use their journal to relate what they are learning to issues raised in other courses or in everyday life. They can reflect on each day's lesson and on their own learning styles and difficulties. Also, they can speculate on how they might adapt what they are learning to future jobs or to problems they see in their current work situation.

Writing assignments are excellent ways to ensure that students fully understand the theories and principles being taught in the course. Writing is also an essential part of the early employment experience of many accountants. Carefully planned assignments can help prepare students for the kinds of writing tasks they will be expected to handle. Obviously one way to be sure that students understand the material in a course is to ask them to write an essay or short answer on an exam. More sophisticated examination approaches could ask students to apply knowledge to a new, unstructured problem or to suggest several solutions to a technical issue.

Many other kinds of writing assignments can help students learn and apply accounting principles. They can be asked to write memos to colleagues or managers about a common problem, or letters to clients describing and justifying an accounting

## THE LEARNING JOURNAL

Students may be asked to keep a learning journal 4-5 days a week throughout the term. A bound notebook is good (less likely to lose pages), though students may prefer their computers. Students may occasionally be given time in class and a specific topic to discuss (i.e., how would you handle the situation described in problem X on page 49). Topics should be related to the course and the profession, but could include reflection on financial news items, ethical dilemmas in business, analysis of learning styles and problems, lists of words and ideas and what they mean, even dialogues with real or historical or imaginary characters.

See Brookfield, *The Skillful Teacher,* for more on the learning journal

change, or reports on specific new Financial Accounting Standards Board rules and their implications for a particular client or company. They can be asked to take one role in a complex case study and discuss the issues from that one perspective. In many of these potential assignments, two key elements come into play: the content of the memo, report, etc., and the audience for which it is intended. Far too many students write for an audience of one - the teacher. They need, instead, to be thinking of a larger, professional audience. Writing assignments in accounting classes should require students to think and write like accountants whose readers will be clients or potential clients or the general public. Assignments should be made as realistic as possible and should be read by classmates as well as instructors in order to broaden the writer's sense of audience.

The accounting instructor's role is to set the writing task, challenge and coach the students, and evaluate the results. Managing all of these writing assignments can be a

## WRITING CLIENT LETTERS

At Adrian College, Accounting Professor Doris de Lespinasse turns problems from the textbook into writing assignments for her students. She asks students to write letters based on "client" questions that arise from problems previously discussed in class. A typical assignment might be: "Company X is your audit client. The president does not understand the adjustment you recommend to capitalize the equipment the company is leasing. Write a letter which explains why accountants treat some leases as sales, why this one must be treated this way, and what effect this will have on Company X's financial statements in the first year." Details about the company are provided in the problem in the text. Students must write for a very specific audience and explain accounting principles to a reader who is not an accountant. The exercise tests their own understanding as well as their writing ability and their sense of audience (de Lespinasse, 1985).

problem, especially if there is only limited assistance with reading and evaluating papers. While we believe it is important for the professor to see some work from every student, it is not necessary to see all of it. Nor is it necessary for every piece of writing to receive a letter grade. Scofield and Combes (1993) and Stocks et al. (1992) offer several alternatives for assigning and grading written work in accounting. Some work can be graded plus or minus, or satisfactory/unsatisfactory, or on a numerical scale of some kind. Some work can be shared in class and discussed with a peer. Some professors ask students to do peer reviews of fellow students' papers, and then the writer edits and revises on the basis of the peer comments. Only the final, polished version is submitted for grading. Whatever the difficulties, and the ingenious ways professors use to overcome them, if students are to learn to communicate effectively in writing, they must write often and well on topics they care about, and their writing must be read, and eventually evaluated.

### 4.3.7 Technology

Like writing, the use of technology as a teaching/learning strategy cuts across all attributes of intentional learning and all courses in the accounting program. Technology may be seen as an accounting tool used in practice, as a teaching tool in the classroom, and as a learning tool to be used by individual students. This section will focus on using technology to enhance teaching and learning, that is, to encourage intentional learning.

Most accounting faculty use some kinds of technology in their courses. In class, the use of film, video, and overhead projectors is common. Some classrooms are now equipped with computers and screen projectors so that students or faculty can work computer problems before the whole class. Many faculty assign problems that must be worked on computers, using either specialized accounting software or spreadsheets. These are all useful ways to assure that future accountants will be comfortable with some of the technology they will encounter in the work place.

To encourage intentional learning, however, the use of technology should go beyond practicing certain accounting techniques or learning to use software or data bases. Students need to be actively engaged in asking questions, analyzing situations, exploring alternatives, solving problems. Technology should be a tool in this activity, not its focus. Kozma and Johnston have described award-winning educational software based on principles of active, not passive, learning. They suggest that using this software, "students become more active and engaged in the learning process; they learn for understanding and application rather than memorization; and they connect their new knowledge to that previously learned, to the ideas of other students, and to the real world outside the classroom" (1991, p. 22). These are the kinds of learning experiences accounting students will need if they are to become effective, independent learners.

Before introducing a new technology, faculty should ask such questions as: What will students learn from this technology? Is this a better way to learn these facts, principles, techniques? What experience or practice will students gain from this technology? What attributes of intentional learning will they be using or developing? Students should also be encouraged to ask these questions about their own learning with technology. The answers to these questions may suggest ways to use technology to enhance learning. Some examples might be:

- A film or video might be used in class to illustrate a topic covered in lecture. How can the instructor ensure that students will be engaged intellectually? One way is to stop the film and ask students to make notes or raise questions or speculate about what will happen next. Another is to engage them in small group discussion after the film.

- Some publishing firms offer computer simulations tied to certain chapters or topics in their textbooks. These may require 10-20 hours of student effort, most of it out of class. Students might be asked to work on these in teams, so that they will question one another, reflect on and articulate what they are learning in the process of doing the exercise. They might also keep a journal of what they are learning individually or as a group.

- An award-winning, computer-based simulation exercise permits students to enter financial decisions into a hypothetical company's accounting information system and to see the effects of those decisions on the financial statements. Students can run the company for up to twenty years, and the program can model real-life consequences including being fired for the bad results of their decisions. The simulation helps students understand how financial decisions interact and how they affect a company's profitability and financial position. (Interactive Financial Statement Simulation, winner of 1990 EDUCOM Distinguished Software Award, Forrest W. Harlow, Jr., Angelo State University, author and publisher.)

- Videos may demonstrate an ethical dilemma in an audit situation or a personnel problem in a work team or a problem faced by a firm's chief financial officer. Such videos could be used for case discussion or written analysis and problem solving.

- Both Arizona State University and the University of Notre Dame use technology to teach basic accounting concepts. At Arizona State, a course required only of accounting majors uses computer-based instruction to teach the preparation of financial accounting information. At Notre Dame, faculty use computer software to teach the accounting (bookkeeping) cycle. Using a manual approach instructors might need four weeks to cover the material; Notre Dame faculty now cover it in about two weeks.

Technology can be used both to present a problem (on transparencies, film, video) and to solve it (using spreadsheets, data bases, computer software). The instructor's role in using technology is to select or create activities and guide students in learning from them. The instructor should lead students to ask questions about how they are solving a problem as well as about the problem itself or the decision to be made. They should be encouraged to reflect on the problem solving process and should be expected to adapt that process to other, different, complex problems. Students should be encouraged to see technology as a tool that helps them learn to learn and to solve the problems they will face in their profession.

## 4.4 The Context of Learning

The environment or context of learning affects the nature and success of the learning experience. This section will review some of the positive and negative influences of environment on learning and suggest some ways that accounting faculty can change and use the educational environment to enhance student learning. We will discuss a range of influences, both physical and psychological, starting with the situation of the class and classroom, moving to the campus culture, and finally considering the discipline and profession of accounting in its role as a context of learning.

The classroom setting is, of course, an obvious and often discouraging context for learning. But the class itself may also be considered as context. By class here we mean the course itself, the teaching/learning activities both during and outside class time, the sequencing or schedule of the class, and the atmosphere of the group. We have discussed course design and teaching strategies in earlier sections. We will consider here the setting, sequencing, and atmosphere of the class.

Ideally, a class is held in a bright, clean, well-equipped room that accommodates every student comfortably. To encourage active learning and student involvement, seats are arranged so students can see each other as well as the instructor. Unfortunately, very few classrooms are ideal settings for learning. Faculty can make some accommodations to enhance the setting of a class. If seats are moveable, they can be rearranged to encourage student interaction; if the room is bare, faculty may bring in visual aids or equipment to make the space more attractive or usable. Meyers and Jones (1993) offer many suggestions for adapting inadequate teaching space.

The sequencing of a class (time of day, class length) is another important element of context. While most institutions mandate 50 or 90 minute classes, many active learning exercises and methods work best in longer sessions. Some faculty may be able to negotiate with administrators for flexibility in scheduling. More feasibly, a group of accounting faculty can explore combining courses for majors into new time frames. Faculty forced to work within a 50-minute class will need to schedule class time carefully, avoiding wasteful preliminary announcements, timing exercises and group work to allow for debriefing, breaking long exercises like complex case studies into logical parts, encouraging students to continue group work and discussions outside of class.

To encourage intentional learning, instructors need to develop an atmosphere of trust and encouragement. The attributes of questioning, organizing, connecting, reflecting, and adapting can be risky behaviors in many highly competitive accounting classes. All too often, students view their classmates as competitors and their teacher as the enemy. Teachers need to help students to be more cooperative than competitive; to see that by helping each other learn they are themselves learning. Focus on learning as a process and goal is one way to encourage a supportive atmosphere. At this point, some readers are probably saying this is coddling the learners. Accounting students can and do survive stressful learning situations. But we doubt that they become lifelong intentional learners in that environment.

To develop a sense of community, participants need common goals and experiences. The accounting instructor should articulate goals for the course that include learning as well as content goals. Students can be encouraged to develop their own goals and to share them with classmates. Although initially it may seem wasteful, time spent developing common goals will lead to cooperative and productive learning later in the course. Common experiences may result from many of the teaching strategies discussed earlier. The teacher who acts as a learning coach, the use of group projects and reports, the sharing of writing exercises and solutions to problems—all promote a positive class atmosphere. Humor, if not forced, or at the expense of specific students, can also be a common bond for a class. The instructor should encourage and demonstrate risk taking and the confidence to learn from trial and error. In an atmosphere where risk is encouraged and error is not fatal, students can be expected to engage in the activities of intentional learning.

---

### CLASS ATMOSPHERE

For an advanced writing class (10-20 juniors and seniors) the instructor prepared coffee and cocoa and the students took turns bringing cookies. The refreshments created only minimal confusion and mess, and students appreciated the sense of camaraderie that sharing food added to the class.

In a large accounting class, the lecturer chose not to wear a microphone. "If students in the back row can't hear," she said, "they'll just have to tell their neighbors to stop talking." Had she troubled to sit in the back row herself, she would have noticed that the combination of distance and a noisy heating system made it almost impossible for students in these seats to participate in the course.

Baxter Magolda's interviewees described a lecturer who made a class of 300 seem much smaller "because he just is so personal.... He moves around a lot, walking up and down the aisles. You know that he wants people to come to class. He cares about students." This instructor came to class early to talk to students. He helped students connect with others in the class to find rides home for holidays. He recognized students as people with interests and lives outside of his class (Baxter Magolda, pp. 279-280).

---

Because large classes are common in accounting education, and because they are the most difficult context for encouraging intentional learning, we now specifically address the context of large classes. Teaching Introduction to Accounting to 500 sophomores is an enormous challenge. It is not surprising that many instructors resort to lecturing and giving objective exams, perhaps supplemented by laboratories or discussion sections. However, the new goals of accounting education call for students to take a more active role in learning than most large courses now permit. Some intentional learning must be introduced in the first courses to begin the process of learning to learn.

The setting for a large class is inevitably a lecture hall. While some business schools have elegant accommodations, even attractive new lecture halls may not be well engineered for learning. Often hot, crowded, and noisy, they are a poor setting for both faculty and students. If the class runs longer than an hour, students may need a break, but the logistics of moving them in and out prevent that option. Faculty need all their ingenuity to deal with such a setting. Instead of a break, they might try a "seventh inning stretch." To provide variety, they might move around in front of and even around the room (wearing a portable microphone, of course). Audio visual aids, demonstrations, learning in pairs and small groups will also help reduce the negative influence of the setting.

Sequencing of large classes offers some opportunity to introduce flexibility. Some faculty plan several occasions during the term when only half the class attends lecture. At the same time, the rest of the class could be meeting in their work or study groups elsewhere on campus. If the lecture is associated with labs or discussion sections, care should be taken to vary the approach between lecture and lab. The lectures could be star performances and could include guest speakers, films, debates, and demonstrations while the discussions offer opportunity for group work, problem solving, and written exercises.

Although difficult to do, a supportive atmosphere can be developed in a large class. One step is for the professor to introduce herself as a person to the class, and share occasional professional experience anecdotes or illustrations (but not a whole semester of war stories!). Another step is to help students learn to know each other. Some faculty ask them to exchange names and phone numbers with 2-3 classmates so they have someone to call if they miss class. Pair learning or group work early in the term will also help students get acquainted. Students need to feel that their instructor is interested in them, at least collectively. Simply arriving early and chatting with students helps send that message. Some faculty hold group office hours or supplemental instruction sessions, some invite students to join them for a snack after class (if all 500 are likely to accept, the invitation could be offered by sections or rows). McKeachie describes using a student feedback committee to meet with him and discuss lectures, exams, and other student concerns. Anything a lecturer can do to show students she cares about them and their learning will help build a sense of trust in the large class.

---

### MANAGING LARGE CLASSES

Some helpful hdeas for managing large classes are distilled into the following list:

1.  Plan ahead—including administrative details.
2.  Prepare thoroughly—problems are magnified in a large class.
3.  Get to know your students—use a survey, visit small groups and discussion sessions, meet with representative students.
4.  Be natural and personal in class—be yourself.
5.  Give clear and thorough instructions for assignments, group work, projects, etc.
6.  Learn to use the computer and other timesaving technology—a computerized guidebook, computer-generated comments on papers or alternate versions of tests.

See McKeachie (1994), Weimer (1987), Erickson and Strommer (1991)

Like class and classroom, institutional culture is an important element in the context of learning. By institutional culture we mean such factors as the institutional type, the institution's historical mission and tradition, the campus culture as evidenced in the values and activities of both faculty and students. Faculty culture is crucial to learning and curriculum change. The institution's values and reward system, the views of key administrators, the demands of the discipline, the faculty member's own professional needs—all shape faculty culture. Faculty who want to change curriculum and teaching methods need to consider the current mood of their colleagues and find ways to address their fears and concerns. The sense of trust desired in the accounting classroom will be even more necessary in the accounting faculty meeting that plans changes in the curriculum.

To achieve emphasis on learning as well as on accounting content, the faculty culture at many institutions must change. Faculty who want to promote intentional learning need to engage colleagues in talk about teaching and learning and the demands of the accounting workplace. There are a number of ways to do this; for example, workshops, faculty meetings, team teaching, visiting classes of colleagues, reading and discussing AECC publications or the results of AECC grant projects. Strategies that have been used by AECC grant schools to encourage change include: bringing recruiters and employers on campus to meet with faculty and students and describe the realities of the workplace; involving outside experts in workshops, retreats, and in mediating difficulties; persuading administrators to reward curriculum innovation and new teaching approaches. Accounting faculty may wish to consult colleagues in other disciplines that traditionally use discussion and other informal teaching styles, or explore problem-oriented teaching in professional schools. Part-time faculty who are full-time accounting practitioners bring immediate experience to the classroom and could be enlisted to help focus on real life problems. They need to be included in the change process so that their courses will be consistent with the rest of the program. Of all the elements of context, faculty culture is one that faculty can and should strongly influence.

For students, the most important context of college life is fellow students. Astin (1993) stresses that "students' values, beliefs, and aspirations tend to change in the direction of the dominant values, beliefs, and aspirations of the peer group" (p. 398). For faculty who teach in an institution where campus life is more important than studies or where students are seeking a career credential with the least possible effort, this is bad news.

Faculty who want to encourage intentional learning need to consider the effect of student values and culture on attitudes toward learning. One approach might be to encourage a subculture of accounting students. Programs that require a high GPA for entry to the major may create a sense that accounting students are serious about their work. Clubs and activities centered around the major might also help create a subculture group. If the campus peer group is a negative influence, faculty need to find creative ways to counter that influence.

The student context becomes particularly important in a time of curricular change. A report on some accounting curriculum change projects pointed out a number of student concerns related to change and suggested some strategies to address them. Students involved in the projects were anxious about the new curriculum—its difficulty, its experimental nature, its effect on their ability to pass the CPA exam and on their future careers. The new program did not meet their expectations of how to learn accounting, expectations based on high school courses and on the experience of other college students. They were upset because "Students in accounting have a disposition for and are at home competing against each other; they work independently and have survived because of their own efforts. The new curriculum urges them to work in groups, to cooperate, to succeed together. This attitude is foreign to their historical style of how to be successful" (Pincus, et al., p. 3). Some programs dealt with these concerns by providing information in orientation, counseling sessions, and open discussions during the term. They brought in employers to tell students (and sometimes parents) why change is needed and what graduates will be expected to know and do. Programs involved in change need to be aware of the student context and to provide information and support to help students develop a positive peer group culture.

As noted earlier, many accounting students begin their course work at two-year schools and transfer to four-year institutions. Both institutions need to take responsibility for easing this transition. Formal articulation agreements are a good start. Faculty may confer on specific courses and perhaps exchange visits. Faculty at both two-year and four-year schools should develop techniques to prepare students to be effective learners. Successful transfer students might visit accounting classes at their two-year school to share their experience.

Another key element in the context of learning accounting is the discipline and profession itself. Faculty interested in promoting the attributes of intentional learning in accounting education need to be aware of the preconceptions students bring to the classroom. Students may enter the field because they are good at numbers; they see the world in a dualistic way and think accounting fits that view; or they expect to memorize and operate within a set of finite rules. These students need to be introduced to a broader image of accounting early in their course work. They need to see possibilities in small practices as well as in Big Six firms, in corporate as well as in public accounting, in the variety of demands made on and talents required of practicing accountants. An understanding of the complexities of the accounting profession will give students a realistic and positive context for learning to learn and learning accounting.

## 4.5 Results and Evaluation

Results and evaluation of the teaching/learning process will be treated together here. By results are meant both the nature and success of the curriculum or course and the learning outcomes of individual students in the program. We begin this section by looking at course results and classroom assessment, that is, at what kind of course best promotes intentional learning and at how such courses may be evaluated. Then we consider student outcomes and the testing and grading practices by which they are evaluated. These practices both measure and affect the learning experience.

### 4.5.1 Course Results and Classroom Assessment

Making learning to learn a course goal means changing how the course is taught and how the students learn. Desirable course results will go beyond a fixed amount of accounting material learned and demonstrated in problems and exams. Course results will also include high levels of attendance and participation, commitment to learning goals, mutual effort and cooperation, conscious practice of and reflection on learning strategies. Course results may also include some noise and confusion, lots of activity, and a sense of energy and involvement in the classroom.

Evaluation of course results will go beyond the usual measurement of how much accounting content students learned and whether they were satisfied with the workload and instruction. Evaluation must be an ongoing activity to assess the learning process, level of student activity and involvement, student understanding, and learning needs. Questions to consider might include: Are students asking questions? Learning to organize knowledge? Seeing connections in what they are learning? Are they thinking instead of just memorizing? Are they engaged with the subject? Involved with one another? Is there a sense of common goals and mutual support in the class? Are the students learning to learn and are they practicing the attributes of intentional learning?

*Classroom Assessment Techniques* (Angelo and Cross, 1993) is an excellent resource for faculty who want to evaluate the quality of the learning experience in their classes. The book consists of three parts: a description of the classroom assessment process, how to begin using it, and twelve successful projects (including one from an Intermediate Financial Accounting course); a section describing fifty successful classroom assessment techniques and how and when to use them; a brief discussion of what has been learned from five years of experience. This handbook is full of specific examples and suggestions from many disciplines and a variety of institutions.

Classroom assessment is to be used throughout the term to evaluate faculty and student learning goals. Some exercises could be used to evaluate how much accounting a student has learned, but focus is on evaluation to improve the course as it progresses. The fifty classroom assessment techniques are organized in the book according to the kinds of teaching/learning goals they best evaluate, for example, course-related knowledge and skills, critical thinking, synthesis and creative thinking, problem solving, learning and study skills. Each assessment technique is presented with a description, purpose, list of related teaching goals, examples, procedures, data analysis, pros and cons and caveats. Indexes list the techniques by discipline (two accounting, nine others in business), by goals and alphabetically. Almost all of the techniques could be adapted for use in accounting classes. Many of the techniques are simple and would take very little time to implement. A few examples that could be particularly useful for accounting faculty will be summarized here:

- The Muddiest Point involves asking students to jot down quickly a response to "What was the muddiest point in..."the lecture, discussion, reading, etc. This technique identifies learning problems and topics the instructor needs to develop. It can be used in even very large classes and it helps students to assess their own problems in learning.
- Two techniques that assess synthesis and creative thinking are the one-sentence summary and approximate analogies. The first requires students to answer "Who does what to whom, when, where, how, and why" about a topic and then to synthesize the answers into a single, grammatical summary sentence. In the second, students must complete the second half of an analogy which the instructor has started, that is, A is to B as ? is to ?. Both of these techniques require students to see relationships and make connections and to present them in a very few words.

- What's the Principle? assesses problem solving skills. This technique requires students to identify the principle used to solve a particular problem. It assesses their ability to relate the general and the specific and to apply principles to new problems.

Faculty across the country and in many disciplines have found classroom assessment an effective way to improve their own teaching and their students' learning. Faculty find that classroom assessment increases student commitment to learning, helps develop a sense of community in the class, improves student satisfaction, and helps students assess their own learning processes, that is, helps them learn to learn. An accounting professor who uses the Minute Paper technique finds that it forces his students to pay attention to their own learning...."I find evidence of focusing on learning in the fact that the quality of questions I receive improves as the semester progresses. That is, the later questions pertain more to accounting techniques or important concepts and less to `right answers' than the earlier questions did. Thus, students, through self-assessment of learning in progress, appear to gain maturity in their learning of accounting" (Cottell, 1991, p. 51).

### 4.5.2 Student Outcomes and Evaluation

The measurement of student outcomes is a major topic in higher education circles today. Our interest is not in the broad outcomes of student development, but in the outcomes of intentional learning: questioning, organizing, connecting, reflecting, adapting. The attributes will be evaluated not by asking students about them, but by asking students to do them while also demonstrating knowledge of accounting principles and practice. The successful student in the new accounting curriculum: asks questions about process and content, organizes new knowledge into logical structures, connects new concepts with known concepts and experience, reflects on new material and on the process of learning it, and adapts knowledge from one context to solve problems in other settings.

Evaluating outcomes like these requires a different approach than that used in many college courses today. Evaluation should match the goals and teaching/learning strategies of the course. Evaluation should include a variety of methods and should occur often and early so that both faculty and students can monitor the success of learning. The AECC-sponsored monograph on assessment (Gainen and Locatelli, 1995) includes many helpful suggestions for evaluating a variety of learning outcomes in accounting courses.

Research shows that students' study habits are influenced by evaluation methods. McKeachie and others report that "...if teachers say that they are concerned about developing skills and strategies for further learning and problem solving and that they hope to help students develop cognitive structures that will form a foundation for continued learning and then give tests that require memory of individual facts, definitions, and isolated information, students will memorize the facts, definitions, and information on which they expect to be tested. In doing so they will use memorization, repetition, and other learning strategies unlikely to be useful for achieving the higher order cognitive objectives we have proclaimed" (McKeachie et al., 1986, p. 76).

One of the most popular methods of evaluating student outcomes is multiple choice exams. This method has several advantages: grading is consistent, reliable, fast and easy; exams can be given efficiently to large classes. The method's disadvantages are that developing really good questions is very time consuming, and it is difficult (but not impossible) to include higher level thinking/learning skills in answering. Students preparing for multiple choice exams are likely to focus on facts and details rather than concepts and their applications. They are not likely to use the attributes of intentional learning in this process.

However, multiple choice exams may be the most practical evaluation method for accounting faculty with large classes. There are ways to broaden multiple choice questions to involve more thinking and less memorizing or guessing. Some faculty permit students to add a rationale for their answers to questions about which they have some uncertainty. A good rationale for a wrong answer may gain some credit and will also require the student to articulate his thinking. Erickson and Strommer (1991) offer suggestions for multiple choice questions that ask students to remember and relate key ideas, recognize ideas or examples in a different context, or apply concepts to new situations. Writing multiple choice questions that require students to analyze and think is not easy, and such questions are not likely to be found in a textbook's standard test bank, but it can be done.

---

### LEARNING THROUGH TESTING

"In cost accounting I didn't get any of the five questions right, but I got an A because I rationalized and explained what I did, even if it wasn't the answer he was looking for. This was the highest form of learning—not just getting one specific answer but understanding everything that went into it and being able to use the pieces to get a result."
Sidney, junior

"Essays are best. They give you a chance to integrate all your thoughts from different areas—...Apply thoughts to a situation. The real world will ask us to apply—not multiple-choice questions."
Stephanie, senior

Comments by transitional knowers in Baxter Magolda,
*Knowing and Reasoning in College,* p. 243

---

One way to balance students' preparation for an exam is to include at least one essay question. This may be a relatively short question, but it should require synthesis or application of learned material, not just recall of lecture notes or readings. Short essay questions may ask students to solve a problem, apply a principle or accounting rule, or describe the consequences of an accounting decision. Some faculty ask students to write answers in small groups which must agree on their response. The value of this experience is in the discussion of the question and answer and development of group process skills. Although they take time to grade, essay questions are valuable evaluation methods because they involve analysis, synthesis, reflection, and the ability to explain a response in writing.

Examinations are not the only method for evaluating student outcomes. Students, especially beginning students, need frequent opportunities to explore and demonstrate how they are learning. Many of the classroom assessment techniques and the teaching strategies discussed in an earlier section can be used to evaluate learning and the learning process. Short written exercises or papers, class projects and presentations, responses to problems and case studies, are all good ways to assess student learning. Accounting faculty should use a variety of methods throughout the term to evaluate and improve the outcomes of student learning.

### 4.5.3  Faculty and Course Evaluation

Many faculty are reluctant to attempt innovations in their teaching because change may result in poor teaching evaluations from students and/or administrators. We recognize the risk involved in change. Not every innovation will succeed and not every student will be happy with the changes suggested here. Yet it is clear that if accounting students are to be prepared to deal with the changes in the profession, accounting professors must risk making changes in accounting education.

Faculty who plan to change their courses should consider meeting with relevant administrators to discuss their plans and reasons. Accounting faculty can point to the demands of the profession and marketplace as reasons for change. They may wish to negotiate support from the dean and/or a modified evaluation process to assess the changes being made. The issues statements of the AECC, particularly Statement No. 1, "AECC Urges Priority for Teaching in Higher Education," and No. 5, "Evaluating and Rewarding Effective Teaching," should be particularly helpful.

We recognize that many accounting faculty must use standard student evaluation forms in their classes. These forms probably will not adequately assess the kinds of learning goals we have been discussing here. Faculty may want to add their own section to the standard form, both to assess the effectiveness of their innovations and to remind students of the goals of the class. Faculty may also remind themselves that the best course is not always the most popular course. The ultimate evaluation of learning to learn as a goal of accounting education will be in the performance of accounting graduates who are lifelong independent learners with successful professional careers.

### 4.6  Teaching for Learning

In the list below, we summarize key recommendations made in this chapter. We hope that accounting faculty will find these useful in implementing the new goals of accounting education.

## TEACHING FOR LEARNING
### Activities for Accounting Education

1. Include learning goals as well as accounting content goals in the curriculum and in each course.
2. Discuss the learning process and learning to learn strategies and attributes to make students conscious of these goals. Teach students to verbalize what they are doing and why they are doing it.
3. Teach students the attributes of intentional learning:
   a. Questions to ask about new accounting material and about their learning experience.
   b. Strategies for organizing new knowledge such as outlining, concept mapping, and diagraming.
   c. Methods for making connections between new information and their own experience and previous knowledge.
   d. Techniques for reflecting on what and how they are learning, such as journal writing, short papers, group discussion of learning exercises.
   e. Strategies for adapting knowledge to different, real-world situations, and for expanding their vision and understanding beyond course work.
4. Use a variety of teaching strategies and roles to involve students actively in their learning; focus the course on student learning rather than on professor teaching.
5. Assign problem-solving and critical thinking exercises which include:
   a. Defining the problem.
   b. Assessing available information.
   c. Identifying assumptions.
   d. Examining potential solutions and their possible consequences.
   e. Adopting and evaluating a solution.
6. Expect students to write often and well in all of their accounting courses and require them to write for a specific accounting-related audience.
7. Create a classroom environment which provides an open and continuous opportunity to discuss both accounting subjects and the learning process. Reduce the fear of being wrong or the fear of dealing with the unfamiliar.
8. Encourage positive student peer group attitudes toward learning and develop peer support systems.
9. Give students plenty of practice in thinking about and doing both learning and accounting.
10. Evaluate student learning processes as well as the accounting content learned.

# Chapter Five
# CHANGING ACCOUNTING EDUCATION

Will the current impetus for change really make a difference in accounting education? Ultimately, that question will be answered on a daily basis by the behavior and attitudes of thousands of accounting faculty and students in classrooms around the country. Introducing a focus on the learning process can be an essential ingredient in the answer. Developing intentional learners who consciously employ the attributes of questioning, organizing, connecting, reflecting, and adapting in any new learning or working situation will make accounting a profession of lifelong learners as well as effective practitioners.

## 5.1 Implementing Learning to Learn

Learning to learn will empower students to do for themselves what they may now expect instructors to do for them. Students will learn to ask their own questions, organize their own knowledge, and reflect on their own learning. To help them, faculty must develop their own approaches to teaching and learning, approaches that fit their students' needs and their own teaching styles and assignments. We will draw upon material presented earlier to suggest some ways to begin implementing learning to learn in accounting classes.

Implementation should begin where the student is. That means considering the student's base of content knowledge, intellectual development, preparation, interests, and aptitude for learning and the profession. In Chapter Three we suggested some ways faculty can learn about their students.

In order to focus our discussion on the elements of learning to learn, we introduced the concept of the intentional learning process. Faculty could begin implementing learning to learn by consciously introducing the five attributes of intentional learning into their accounting courses. They could discuss the attributes with students and involve students in assignments that require them to practice one or more of the attributes.

An educational program designed to teach intentional learning should take a developmental approach; that is, it should begin with relatively simple questions, problems and learning skills, and build to the more sophisticated practices of the independent learner. Faculty could use the elements of the academic plan, discussed in Chapter Four, to facilitate program planning.

Accounting faculty could begin to implement learning to learn by focusing on one approach or aspect of the learning process. They might work with a colleague to develop expertise and share ideas. The goal is to increase student awareness of learning processes. Any one of the following approaches could lead to productive discussion and improvement of student learning.

- Start with the issue of intellectual development. Study Perry or Belenky or Baxter Magolda and apply the developmental approach to classes. Consider student differences and patterns of development. This approach would lead to awareness of differences among freshmen, sophomores, juniors, seniors. It would result in courses planned to support and challenge students to move forward in their intellectual development. It could shape teaching and evaluation methods at each course level.

- Start with the question of learning style. For example, review the Kolb model with students, help them identify their learning preferences, structure assignments to cover the whole cycle of Kolb's experiential learning model, discuss with students the purpose of each part of the learning experience.
- Start with the question of personal characteristics. Use the Myers-Briggs Personality Type Indicator to identify student types. Discuss the implications of personal preferences for learning and give students conscious practice in using both their preferred and not preferred approaches to learning.
- Start with a discussion of course goals. Discuss the goals on your syllabus, and ask students to articulate their own goals. Share these in class, discuss any differences, and explain how course activities will address course goals. Expect students to take responsibility for the learning goals they set.
- Concentrate on introducing active learning experiences in your course, using projects, groups, pairs, games, simulations, or case studies. Discuss with students why they are being asked to undertake these activities.

Accounting faculty may choose among these approaches depending upon their own interests and their students' characteristics. The developmental approach will work best in a relatively homogeneous class where most students are of traditional college age. The learning style and personality type approaches would work well with any age student. These three approaches will require the accounting instructor to develop some expertise outside her field. Accounting programs might introduce these approaches as team efforts or faculty development projects. The course goal and active learning approaches may be more immediately accessible to accounting faculty. These approaches could easily be adopted by individual faculty.

## 5.2 Problems to Consider

We review now some potential problems of implementing change in the accounting curriculum as we have encountered them and as faculty engaged in change efforts have shared them with us. We present these problems as they affect the people most directly involved—students, faculty, and administrators of accounting programs.

Students may have problems adjusting to the responsibilities of intentional learning. Particularly at first, they may try to force faculty back into the role of authority and truth teller so they can revert to being passive students. They may resist the active roles of learners, such as working in groups and sharing questions and knowledge with their peers. They are more accustomed to individual effort and competition. With patience and clear communication of the rationale for change, however, most students will make the necessary adjustment.

Students may need to be persuaded of the validity of a new curriculum. They will have heard from parents, older siblings, friends in the profession that accounting education should include certain experiences. Many will be thinking about passing the

CPA exam and worrying that they won't be learning what they need to know. They will be expecting older style accounting education and may resist change, especially if faculty seem to be experimenting. Faculty need to assure students that accounting content is not being abandoned but is being enhanced by attention to the learning process.

Students may complain about grading practices, particularly if these are different from what has been done in the past. They will raise the flag of <u>fairness</u>. In truth, programs undergoing change have found grading to be a problem. Grading group work, communication and interpersonal skills, the learning itself, are all more difficult than simply testing specific accounting knowledge. Yet if these new skills are to be major objectives of the program, they need to be assessed, for evaluation of the program as much as for the information and transcripts of students.

As discussed in Chapter Three, some students may not be developmentally ready for the responsibility of intentional learning. They may need to be brought along by a combination of challenge and support to develop the intellectual maturity necessary for independent learners. Faculty can help by acquainting themselves with the needs of students at different developmental positions and by planning courses and programs to accommodate those needs.

Faculty may have problems accepting the new teaching role of facilitator/coach/mentor rather than authority/lecturer. It is not easy for the professor who enjoys dispensing knowledge to give up control in order to empower students to take responsibility for their own learning. Faculty will need preparation and encouragement to undertake these new roles. Many colleges and universities sponsor workshops or teaching/learning centers to help faculty learn new approaches to teaching. Faculty in programs where team teaching has been introduced have complained about loss of control over "their" course and "their" students. On the other hand, once they adapted to change, faculty have found benefits in teamwork and in sharing ideas about teaching; they have been energized by work with associates. Course planning done together is often done earlier and more consciously; exams and assignments planned jointly get extra scrutiny and the advantage of advance effort. The new faculty role can be very rewarding when faculty adapt themselves to it.

A major problem for many faculty in revised programs is selection and/or development of course materials. Textbook authors and publishers often resist change that reduces demand for their books. Faculty who want to use innovative approaches have difficulty finding texts and other materials to meet their needs. Many have developed their own course materials. The results can be very satisfying, but the investment of time and energy is significant.

A major concern for faculty who wish to introduce learning to learn into their accounting courses is finding the right balance between content and process. Clearly, giving attention in class to the attributes of intentional learning will mean less class time for the principles and procedures of accounting. There is, as yet, no consensus on what the balance between accounting content and learning process should be. Faculty need to face this issue early in their planning and be ready to adjust the balance as they work through their program changes.

Like students, faculty are concerned about evaluation—of their teaching, their courses, their program. The change process should be designed to protect faculty, especially untenured faculty, from the hazards of trying innovations that may not be successful. Faculty who introduce innovations into their courses need to be in a position to risk failure. They need time and support to adjust, learn what works, change what doesn't. Providing appropriate incentives and safeguards for faculty to participate in change efforts should be part of the planning for change.

Administrators, as well as students and faculty, will encounter problems as they implement changes in the accounting curriculum. New programs require time and resources for planning, implementing, and evaluating changes. Funding will be a significant problem at many institutions where budgets are already tight. The support of deans and central administrators will be crucial to the success of change efforts.

A problem encountered at every point in the change process is communication. All parties—students, faculty, administrators, parents, employers—need to be informed of the rationale, the plans, the process of change. Planning for change must include planning for clear and frequent communication that shows why curriculum change is necessary to prepare accounting graduates for success in the profession.

### 5.3  Using Intentional Learning in Accounting Practice

Robert Elliott, assistant to the chairman of KPMG Peat Marwick and former AECC member, maintains that new accounting practitioners "must be prepared to learn effectively under time pressure in unique situations as well as to maintain and increase the usable knowledge at [their] command. Auditors and consultants, for example, get on a job and must learn immediately, in considerable depth, and without the benefit of a teacher, the client's business and needs. They must learn the latest in business practices and the changing course of the general economy and the client's industry, and they must learn and understand how such conditions affect the client's operations. None of these learning needs can be satisfied by having acquired rules and facts and techniques to apply them."*

New practitioners will find the intentional learning process a helpful approach to the learning needs Elliott describes. As students using the attributes, they will have learned how to learn accounting content. As practitioners, they will consciously use the five attributes on the job to learn about clients and their needs. For example, they can learn about a client's business situation by asking probing questions and organizing the answers into meaningful information. They can connect theory and research with the client's problems and adapt solutions to fit new situations. Having used intentional learning as students, they have a process and a variety of strategies to use in practice. They can be independent learners in the client's office as well as in their own.

Intentional learning provides a base for a variety of skills and knowledge needed by new practitioners. For example, accounting professionals need good reading skills to understand complex laws and rulings they may encounter in their work. They may use the attributes of questioning, connecting, and reflecting as they analyze and interpret what they are reading. New practitioners need to use the accounting research skills they acquired in their accounting courses. They can use questioning, organizing, and adapting as they research problems for their clients. New practitioners need to analyze

---

*Letter to Richard E. Flaherty, Executive Director, AECC, April 5, 1994.

what they are learning and to make judgments, including ethical judgments, about information they acquire and how to use it. The whole accounting degree program, including general and business as well as accounting education, should help students develop these abilities. The intentional learning process, consciously used in accounting practice, will help a new professional learn to meet her client's or employer's needs.

Successful accounting professionals need intellectual maturity to be independent learners. As discussed in Chapter Three, many graduating seniors have not yet achieved the maturity necessary to think and learn independently. New practitioners must be challenged and supported to continue their intellectual development. Using and reflecting on the intentional learning process in their work will encourage them to be independent learners.

The early employment experience of new practitioners will be crucial to their continuing development. The AECC recognized the importance of this experience in its Issues Statement No. 4, "Improving the Early Employment Experience of Accountants." The statement urged supervisors to be strong leaders and mentors for new hires and to provide stimulating work assignments that offer opportunities to exercise a broad range of skills. The statement also urged employers to provide educational experiences that reinforce skills and meet employee needs. Faculty who use intentional learning in their programs might share their experience with employers and encourage attention to the attributes of learning in the employment setting.

A major goal of the AECC is to empower accounting graduates to learn on their own: on the job, in the library, through experience and consultation with clients and fellow professionals. New accounting practitioners need a broad view of knowledge and learning, need to be aware of their own styles, strengths, and weaknesses as learners, need to be able to use the attributes of intentional learning to become independent learners. This monograph is one step in addressing the goal. Adapting the process of intentional learning to accounting courses and programs is another step. Achieving the goal will require that accounting education continue beyond formal instruction to become lifelong, independent, self-education in accounting practice.

# GLOSSARY

Recognizing that many of the terms used to refer to the elements of learning to learn have a variety of meanings depending on context and perspective, we offer here our definitions of some key terms. These definitions represent our best understanding of these words as we are using them in this monograph.

*Active Learning* - is a process of exploring, analyzing, communicating, or using new information or experience.

*Analytical thinking* - is separating and distinguishing elements of a concept (idea, problem, etc.) in order to understand its essential nature and inner relationships.

*Cognition* - is the process by which a person learns; it involves strategies for processing information, prior knowledge about content, and problem-solving and thinking skills.

*Critical thinking* - is exploring questions about and solutions for issues which are not clearly defined and for which there are no clear-cut answers.

*Creativity* - is the ability to produce something new, to generate unique approaches and solutions to issues or problems or opportunities.

*Intentional learning* - is learning with self-directed purpose, intending and choosing to learn and how and what to learn.

*Knowledge* - is facts, information, content.

*Learning* - is the process of developing a skill or of acquiring knowledge and understanding of a subject.

*Learning to learn* - is a process of acquiring, understanding, and using a variety of strategies to improve one's ability to attain and apply knowledge, a process which results from, leads to, and enhances a questioning spirit and a lifelong desire to learn.

*Learning strategies* - are cognitive processes students use to learn, understand, and apply material that may be relatively complex, e.g., summarizing the key points in a textbook chapter).

*Learning style* - is the combination of individual characteristics (personal, psychological, intellectual) that shape a student's approach to a learning task.

*Metacognition* - is thinking about thinking and knowing about knowing, being aware of and controlling the learning process.

*Motivation* - is student's reason for learning and may be personal (intrinsic) or external (extrinsic).

*Problem solving* - is thinking about and finding answers for a relatively clearly-defined situation for which there are one or more reasonable answers.

*Study skills* - are very basic techniques for learning relatively unsophisticated material (i.e. mnemonics for memorizing lists or the multiplication tables).

# REFERENCES AND RESOURCES

Accounting Education Change Commission (AECC). 1990 (August). *Issues Statement No. 1:* AECC Urges Priority for Teaching in Higher Education.

Accounting Education Change Commission (AECC). 1993 (April). *Issues Statement No. 5:* Evaluating and Rewarding Effective Teaching.

Accounting Education Change Commission (AECC). 1993 (April). *Issues Statement No. 4:* Improving the Early Employment Experience of Accountants.

Accounting Education Change Commission (AECC). 1992 (August). *Issues Statement No. 3:* The Importance of Two-Year Colleges for Accounting Education.

Accounting Education Change Commission (AECC). 1990 (September). *Position Statement No. 1*: Objectives of Education for Accountants.

Accounting Education Change Commission (AECC). 1992 (June). *Position Statement No. 2:* The First Course in Accounting.

Ainsworth, Penne L. and Plumlee, David R. 1993 (Spring). Restructuring the Accounting Curriculum Sequence: The KSU Experience." *Issues in Accounting Education,* 8(1), 112-127.

American Accounting Association Committee on the Future Content, Structure and Scope of Accounting Education (The Bedford Committee). 1986 (Spring). Future Accounting Education: Preparing for the Expanded Profession. *Issues in Accounting Education,* 1(1), 168-195.

American Institute of Certified Public Accountants (AICPA). 1991. *Accounting Recruiting Research: Survey of High School and College Students, 1990-91*. New York: Author.

Angelo, Thomas A. and Cross, K. Patricia. 1993. *Classroom Assessment Techniques: A Handbook for College Teachers*. San Francisco, CA: Jossey-Bass.

Arthur Andersen & Co., Arthur Young, Coopers & Lybrand, Deloitte Haskins & Sells, Ernst & Whinney, Peat Marwick Main & Co., Price Waterhouse, and Touche Ross. 1989 (April). *Perspectives on Education: Capabilities for Success in the Accounting Profession*. New York: Authors.

Ashworth, John. 1968 (November). People Who Become Accountants. *The Journal of Accountancy.* No volume. 43-49.

Association of American Colleges (AAC). 1990. *The Challenge of Connecting Learning*. Washington, D.C.: AAC.

Astin, Alexander W. 1993. *What Matters in College: Four Critical Years Revisited*. San Francisco, CA: Jossey-Bass.

Barrows, H.S. and Tamblyn, R.N. 1980. *Problem-Based Learning: An Approach to Medical Education*. New York: Springer.

Baxter Magolda, Marcia B. 1992. *Knowing and Reasoning in College*. San Francisco, CA: Jossey-Bass.

Belenky, Mary Field, Clinchy, Blythe McVicker, Goldberger, Nancy Rule, and Tarule, Jill Mattuck. 1986. *Women's Ways of Knowing: The Development of Self, Voice & Mind*. New York: Basic Books.

Bloom, Benjamin S. (Ed.). 1956. *Taxonomy of Educational Objectives: The Classification of Educational Goals, by a Committee of College and University Examiners.* Handbook I, Cognitive Domain. New York: Longmans, Green.

Brigham Young University Integrated Junior Year Accounting Core. 1992. *Report to the AECC.* Provo, UT: Brigham Young University.

Brookfield, Stephen D. 1987. *Developing Critical Thinkers: Challenging Adults to Explore Alternative Ways of Thinking and Acting.* San Francisco, CA: Jossey-Bass.

Brookfield, Stephen D. 1990. *The Skillful Teacher: On Technique, Trust, and Responsiveness in the Classroom.* San Francisco, CA: Jossey-Bass.

Candy, Philip C. 1991. *Self-Direction for Lifelong Learning: A Comprehensive Guide to Theory and Practice.* San Francisco, CA: Jossey-Bass.

Canfield, Albert. 1988. *Learning Styles Inventory Manual.* Los Angeles, CA: Western Psychological Services.

Carpenter, Vivian L., Friar, Shirley, and Lipe, Marlys Gascho. 1993 (Spring). Evidence on the Performance of Accounting Students: Race, Gender, and Expectations. *Issues in Accounting Education,* 8(1), 1-17.

Christensen, C. Roland, Garvin, David A., and Sweet, Ann. (Eds). 1991. *Education for Judgment: The Artistry of Discussion Leadership.* Cambridge, MA: Harvard Business School.

Christensen, C. Roland and Hansen, Abby J. 1987. *Teaching and the Case Method.* Boston, MA: Harvard Business School.

Claxton, Charles S. and Murrell, Patricia H. 1987. *Learning Styles: Implications for Improving Educational Practices.* ASHE-ERIC Higher Education Report No. 4. Washington, D.C.: The George Washington University.

Cory, Suzanne. 1992 (Spring). Quality and Quantity of Accounting Students and the Stereotypical Accountant: Is There a Relationship?" *Journal of Accounting Education,* 10(1), 1-24.

Cottell, Philip G., Jr. 1991 (Summer). Classroom Research in Accounting: Assessing for Learning. In Thomas A. Angelo (Ed.) *Classroom Research: Early Lessons from Success.* New Directions for Teaching and Learning. No. 46. San Francisco, CA: Jossey-Bass.

Davidson, Ronald A. 1991 (September). Straw Accountants. *CA Magazine,* 124(9), 43-47.

Davis, Barbara Gross. 1993. *Tools for Teaching.* San Francisco, CA: Jossey-Bass.

Davis, James R. 1993. *Better Teaching, More Learning: Strategies for Success in Postsecondary Settings.* Phoeniz, AZ: American Council on Education and Oryx Press.

Davis, Todd M. and Murrell, Patricia H. 1993. *Turning Teaching Into Learning: The Role of Student Responsibility in the Collegiate Experience.* ASHE-ERIC Higher Education Report No. 8. Washington, D.C.: George Washington University, School of Education and Human Development.

DeCoster, Don T. and Rhode, John Grant. 1971 (October). The Accountant's Stereotype: Real or Imagined, Deserved or Unwarranted. *The Accounting Review,* XLVI(4), 651-663.

de Lespinasse, Doris. 1985 (Spring). Writing Letters to Clients: Connecting Textbook Problems and the Real World. *Journal of Accounting Education,* 3(1), 197-200.

Deppe, Larry A., Sonderegger, Emory O., Stice, James O., Clark, D. Cecil, and Streuling, G. Fred. 1991 (Fall). Emerging Competencies for the Practice of Accountancy. *Journal of Accounting Education,* 9(2), 257-290.

Diamond, Robert M. 1989. *Designing and Improving Courses and Curricula in Higher Education: A Systematic Approach.* San Francisco, CA: Jossey-Bass.

Erickson, Bette L. and Strommer, Diane W. 1991. *Teaching College Freshmen.* San Francisco, CA: Jossey-Bass.

Frecka, Thomas J. 1992. *Critical Thinking, Interactive Learning, and Technology: Reaching for Excellence in Business Education.* Arthur Andersen & Co.

Frederick, Peter J. 1986 (Spring). The Lively Lecture — 8 Variations. *College Teaching,* 34(2), 43-50.

Frederick, Peter J. 1981 (Summer). The Dreaded Discussion: Ten Ways to Start. *Improving College and University Teaching,* 29(3), 109-114.

Fuhrmann, Barbara S. and Grasha, Anthony F. 1983. *A Practical Handbook for College Teachers.* Boston, MA: Little Brown & Co.

Gainen, Joanne and Locatelli, Paul. 1995. *Assessment for the New Curriculum: A Guide for Professional Accounting Programs.* Accounting Education Series, Volume No. 11. Sarasota, FL: American Accounting Association.

Geary, William T. and Rooney, Cynthia T. 1993 (Spring). Designing Accounting Education to Achieve Balanced Intellectual Development. *Issues in Accounting Education,* 8(1), 60-70.

Inman, Brent, Wenzler, Andre, and Wickert, Peter D. 1989 (Spring). Square Pegs in Round Holes: Are Accounting Students Well-Suited to Today's Accounting Profession? *Issues in Accounting Education,* 4(1), 29-47.

Jacoby, Philip. 1981. Psychological Types and Career Success in the Accounting Profession, *Research on Psychological Type,* 24-37.

Johnson, David W., Johnson, Roger T., and Smith, Karl A. 1991. *Cooperative Learning: Increasing College Faculty Instructional Productivity.* ASHE-ERIC Higher Education Report No. 4. Washington, D.C.: The George Washington University.

King, Patricia M. and Kitchener, Karen Strohm. 1994. *Developing Reflective Judgment: Understanding and Promoting Intellectual Growth and Critical Thinking in Adolescents and Adults.* San Francisco, CA: Jossey-Bass.

King, Patricia M., Kitchener, Karen Strohm, and Wood, Philip K. 1985. The Development of Intellect and Character: A Longitudinal-Sequential Study of Intellectual and Moral Development in Young Adults. *Moral Education Forum,* 10(1), 1-13.

King, Patricia M., Wood, Phillip K., and Mines, Robert A. 1990 (Winter). Critical Thinking Among College and Graduate Students. *The Review of Higher Education,* 13(2), 167-186.

Knechel, W. Robert, 1992 (Fall). Using the Case Method in Accounting Instruction. *Issues in Accounting Education,* 7(2), 205-217.

Knechel, W. Robert and Rand, Richard S. 1994 (Summer). Will the AECC's Course Delivery Recommendations Work in the Introductory Accounting Course? Some Preliminary Evidence. *Journal of Accounting Education,* 12(3), 175-191.

Kolb, David. 1981. Learning Styles and Disciplinary Differences. In Chickering, A.W. (Ed.) *The Modern American College: Responding to the New Realities of Diverse Students and a Changing Society,* 232-252. San Francisco, CA: Jossey-Bass.

Kozma, Robert B. and Johnston, Jerome. 1991 (January/February). The Technological Revolution Comes to the Classroom. *Change,* 23(1), 10-23.

Kurfiss, Joanne Gainen. 1988. *Critical Thinking: Theory, Research, Practice, and Possibilities.* ASHE-ERIC Higher Education Report No. 2. Washington, D.C.: The George Washington University.

Lovell-Troy, Larry and Eickmann, Paul. 1992. *Course Design for College Teachers.* Englewood Cliffs, NJ: Educational Technology Publications.

McKeachie, W.J., P.R. Pintrich, Y. Lin, and D.A.F. Smith, *Teaching and Learning in the College Classroom: A Review of the Research Literature* (Ann Arbor, MI: National Center for Research to Improve Postsecondary Teaching and Learning, The University of Michigan, 1986).

McKeachie, Wilbert J., Pintrich, Paul R., Lin, Yi-Guang, and Smith, David A.F. 1986. *Teaching and Learning in the College Classroom: A Review of the Research Literature.* Ann Arbor, MI: National Center for Research to Improve Postsecondary Teaching and Learning, The University of Michigan.

McKeachie, Wilbert J., Pintrich, Paul R., and Lin, Yi-Guang. 1985 (Summer). Teaching Learning Strategies. *Educational Psychologist,* 20(3), 153-160.

McKeachie, Wilbert J. 1994. *Teaching Tips: A Guidebook for the Beginning College Teacher.* (9th Edition). Lexington, MA: D.C. Heath.

Meyers, Chet and Jones, Thomas B. 1993. *Promoting Active Learning: Strategies for the College Classroom.* San Francisco, CA: Jossey-Bass.

Meyers, Chet. *Teaching Students to Think Critically.* San Francisco: Jossey-Bass.

Myers, Isabel Briggs, 1976. *Myers-Briggs Type Indicator.* Palo Alto, CA: Consulting Psychologists Press.

Paris, Scott G., Lipson, Marjorie Y., and Wixson, Karen K. 1983. Becoming a Strategic Reader. *Contemporary Educational Psychology,* 8(3), 293-316.

Perry, William G., Jr. 1970. *Forms of Intellectual and Ethical Development in the College Years: A Scheme.* New York: Holt, Rinehart and Winston.

Pincus, Karen, Scott, Larry, Searfoss, Jerry, and Clark, Cecil. 1993. *Transitioning for Change: Summary of Interview Data from Twelve Schools.* Unpublished document distributed at meeting of the AECC.

Richardson, Richard C. 1985 (May/June). How Are Students Learning? *Change,* 17(3), 43-49.

Schon, Donald A. 1987. *Educating the Reflective Practitioner: Toward A New Design for Teaching and Learning in the Professions.* San Francisco, CA: Jossey-Bass.

Schon, Donald A. 1983. *The Reflective Practitioner: How Professionals Think in Action.* New York: Basic Books.

Schroeder, Charles C. 1993 (September/October). New Students — New Learning Styles. *Change,* 25(4), 21-26.

Scofield, Barbara W. and Combes, Linda. 1993 (Spring). Designing and Managing Meaningful Writing Assignments. *Issues in Accounting Education,* 8(1), 71-85.

Smith, Robert M. 1992 (December/January). What College Didn't Teach You. *Insight,* 41(7), 26-29.

Smith, Robert M., and Associates. 1990. *Learning to Learn Across the Life Span.* San Francisco, CA: Jossey-Bass.

Stark, Joan S. and Lowther, Malcolm A. 1986. *Designing the Learning Plan: A Review of Research Theory Related to College Curricula.* Ann Arbor, MI: National Center for Research to Improve Postsecondary Teaching and Learning, The University of Michigan.

Stark, Joan S., Lowther, Malcolm A., and Hagerty, Bonnie M.K. 1986. *Responsive Professional Education: Balancing Outcomes and Opportunities.* ASHE-ERIC Higher Education Report No. 3. Washington, D.C.: The George Washington University and Association for the Study of Higher Education.

Stark, Joan S., Lowther, Malcolm A., Shaw, Kathleen M., and Sossen, Paula L. 1991. *Student Goals Exploration User's Manual: Classroom Research Guide.* Ann Arbor, MI: National Center for Research to Improve Postsecondary Teaching and Learning, The University of Michigan.

Stark, Joan S., Lowther, Malcolm A., Bentley, Richard J., Ryan, Michael P., Martens, Gretchen G., Genthon, Michele, Wren, Patricia A., and Shaw, Kathleen M. 1989. *Planning Introductory College Courses: Influences on Faculty.* Ann Arbor, MI: National Center for Research to Improve Postsecondary Teaching and Learning, The University of Michigan.

Stocks, Kevin D., Stoddard, Ted D., and Waters, Max L. 1992 (Fall). Writing in the Accounting Curriculum: Guidelines for Professors. *Issues in Accounting Education,* 7(2), 193-204.

Stout, David E. and Ruble, Thomas L. 1991 (Spring). The Learning Style Inventory and Accounting Education Research: A Cautionary View and Suggestions for Future Research. *Issues in Accounting Education,* 6(1), 41-52.

Svinicki, Marilla D. and Dixon, Nancy M. 1987 (Fall). Kolb Model Modified for Classroom Activities. *College Teaching,* 35(4), 141-146.

Tobias, Sheila, Dougherty, Ralph, and Raphael, Jacqueline. 1994 (February). The Contract Alternative: An Experiment in Teaching and Assessment in Undergraduate Science. *AAHE Bulletin,* 46(6), 3-6.

Weimer, Maryellen G. 1987. *Teaching Large Classes Well.* New Directions for Teaching and Learning, No. 32. San Francisco, CA: Jossey-Bass.

Weinstein, Claire E. and Underwood, Vicki L. 1985. Learning Strategies: The How of Learning. In Segal, Judith W., Chipman, Susan F., and Glaser, Robert. (Eds.) *Thinking and Learning Skills: Relating Instruction to Research,* Vol. I, 241-258. Hillsdale, NJ: Lawrence Erlbaum Associates.

Whitman, Neal A. 1988. *Peer Teaching: To Teach is to Learn Twice.* ASHE-ERIC Higher Education Report No. 4. Washington, D.C.: The George Washington University.

Williams, Doyle Z. 1993 (February 8). The Future of Accounting Education. A presentation to the Administrators of Accounting Programs Group of the American Accounting Association. Las Vegas, Nevada.

Wyer, Jean C. 1984 (Spring). Conceptual v. Procedural: A Developmental Approach. *Journal of Accounting Education,* 2(1), 5-18.

# APPENDIX A
# LEARNING TO LEARN[a]

Learning is often defined and measured in terms of knowledge of facts, concepts, or principles. This "transfer of knowledge" approach to education has been the traditional focus of accounting education. One goal of the Accounting Education Change Commission is to change the educational focus from knowledge acquisition to "learning to learn," that is, developing in students the motivation and capacity to continue to learn outside the formal educational environment. Learning to learn involves developing skills and strategies that help one learn more effectively and to use these effective learning strategies to continue to learn throughout his or her lifetime.

Academic programs focused on teaching students how to learn must address three issues: 1) content, 2) process, and 3) attitudes.

The content of the program must create a base upon which continued learning can be built. Developing both an understanding of underlying concepts and principles and the ability to apply and adapt those concepts and principles in a variety of contexts and circumstances are essential to life-long learning. A focus on memorization of rules and regulations is contrary to the goal of learning to learn.

The process of learning should focus on developing the ability to identify problems and opportunities, search out the desired information, analyze and interpret the information, and reach a well reasoned conclusion. Understanding the process of inquiry in an unstructured environment is an important part of learning to learn.

Above all, an attitude of continual inquiry and life-long learning is essential for learning to learn. An attitude of accepting, even thriving on, uncertainty and unstructured situations should be fostered. An attitude of seeking continual improvement, both of self and the profession, will lead to life-long learning.

---

[a]AECC, *Position Statement No. 1*, p. 6.

## APPENDIX B
## COMPOSITE PROFILE OF CAPABILITIES NEEDED
## BY ACCOUNTING GRADUATES[a]

1. General Knowledge
   - An understanding of the flow of ideas and events in history and the different cultures in today's world
   - Basic knowledge of psychology, economics, mathematics through calculus, and statistics
   - A sense of the breadth of ideas, issues, and contrasting economic, political and social forces in the world
   - An awareness of personal and social values and of the process of inquiry and judgment
   - An appreciation of art, literature, and science

2. Intellectual Skills
   - Capacities for inquiry, abstract logical thinking, inductive and deductive reasoning, and critical analysis
   - Ability to identify and solve unstructured problems in unfamiliar settings and to apply problem-solving skills in a consultative process
   - Ability to identify ethical issues and apply a value-based reasoning system to ethical questions
   - Ability to understand the determining forces in a given situation and to predict their effects
   - Ability to manage sources of stress by selecting and assigning priorities within restricted resources and to organize work to meet tight deadlines

3. Interpersonal Skills
   - Ability to work with others, particularly in groups, to influence them, to lead them, to organize and delegate tasks, to motivate and develop people, and to withstand and resolve conflict
   - Ability to interact with culturally and intellectually diverse people

4. Communication Skills
   - Ability to present, discuss, and defend views effectively through formal and informal, written and spoken language
   - Ability to listen effectively
   - Ability to locate, obtain, organize, report, and use information from human, print, and electronic sources

5. Organizational and Business Knowledge
   - A knowledge of the activities of business, government, and nonprofit organizations, and of the environments in which they operate, including the major economic, legal, political, social, and cultural forces and their influences

---

[a]AECC, *Position Statement No. 1*, pp. 7-8.

- A basic knowledge of finance, including financial statement analysis, financial instruments, and capital markets, both domestic and international
- An understanding of interpersonal and group dynamics in business
- An understanding of the methods for creating and managing change in organizations
- An understanding of the basic internal workings of organizations and the application of this knowledge to specific examples

6. Accounting Knowledge
   - History of the accounting profession and accounting thought
   - Content, concepts, structure, and meaning of reporting for organizational operations, both for internal and external use, including the information needs of financial decision makers and the role of accounting information in satisfying those needs
   - Policy issues, environmental factors, and the regulation of accounting
   - Ethical and professional responsibilities of an accountant
   - The process of identifying, gathering, measuring, summarizing, and analyzing financial data in business organizations, including:
     - The role of information systems
     - The concepts and principles of information system design and use
     - The methods and processes of information system design and use
     - The current and future roles of computer-based information technology
   - The concepts, methods, and processes of control that provide for the accuracy and integrity of financial data and safeguarding of business assets
   - The nature of attest services and the conceptual and procedural bases for performing them
   - Taxation and its impact on financial and managerial decisions
   - In-depth knowledge in one or more specialized areas, such as financial accounting, management accounting, taxation, information systems, auditing, nonprofit, government, and international accounting

7. Accounting Skills
   - Ability to apply accounting knowledge to solve real-world problems

8. Personal Capacities and Attitudes
   - Creative thinking
   - Integrity
   - Energy
   - Motivation
   - Persistence
   - Empathy
   - Leadership
   - Sensitivity to social responsibilities
   - A commitment to life-long learning

**APPENDIX C**
**ASSESSING LEARNING-TO-LEARN SKILLS[a]**

| OBJECTIVE | PERFORMANCE CRITERIA | MEASUREMENT INDICATORS | MEASUREMENT STRATEGIES |
|---|---|---|---|
| **Questioning:** Students actively and effectively use questions to advance their understanding of a subject | Students' questions require analysis, synthesis, application, integration, or evaluation of knowledge | Cognitive complexity of students' questions based on levels of Bloom's taxonomy or "levels-of-processing" theory | Rate students' questions in class discussion<br><br>Rate questions submitted by students in preparation for a major project |
| **Organizing:** Students effectively organize information for storage (retention) and subsequent retrieval | Students' organizing strategies accurately represent relationships among concepts. Students use a variety of organizing strategies for different purposes. | Appropriateness and variety in students' use of organizing strategies (outlines, matrices, flow charts, diagrams, charts, graphs, etc.) | Rate organizational strategies in students' oral and written presentations |
| **Connecting:** Students actively link new concepts and principles to prior learning and experience | Students identify linkages that accurately reflect concepts and advance understanding of accounting situations | Ratings of quality, fluency and appropriateness of linkages between concepts and prior learning or experiences | Rate key-word lists, concept maps, responses on paired concepts tests (quality of relationships identified for a given pair of terms or phrases) |
| **Reflecting:** Students reflect on what they have learned and on their own learning processes | Students demonstrate ability to extract lessons from experiences and to describe their own learning processes | Ratings of quality and appropriateness of reflective observations | Rate debriefing summaries from case discussions and simulations; rate comments in learning journals or self-assessments of strengths and weaknesses in performance on major projects |
| **Adapting:** Students use what they have learned to create new solutions to unstructured problems | Knowledge base is accurate and appropriate; solution proposals are plausible and inventive | Ratings of accuracy and appropriateness of knowledge application; ratings of solution effectiveness and inventiveness | Rate solutions to unstructured case studies, responses in simulations, project proposals, etc. |

[a]Gainen and Locatelli, p. 106.

## APPENDIX D
## EXPERIENCES FROM THE FIELD

This appendix includes some experiences, suggestions, and successful practices of accounting faculty who have attempted curricular change. Most of these examples are related to AECC grant projects or have been shared by readers of this monograph. We invite new readers to share their own experiences with the publisher of this monograph.

### The University of Notre Dame

Thomas J. Frecka, Professor of Accountancy, suggests three problems to avoid in making curricular changes:

1. At the sophomore level, in a rush to build a discovery learning framework into courses, Notre Dame initially used too many complex case studies and too many group assignments. At the introductory level it is important to build a content infrastructure (vocabulary, definitions, etc.). The key is to move students to a higher plane of learning as quickly as possible, using an appropriate blend of challenges and supports.
2. The learning to learn approach is more time-consuming. One way to teach basic skills more efficiently (leaving more class time for developing higher order skills) is through the use of technology. Notre Dame uses computer software to teach the accounting (bookkeeping) cycle.
3. Being the "Lone Ranger" can be a problem. If you are one of only a few people on your faculty who have adopted a new approach, your class may not be popular for some students. The reason is that a learning to learn approach, at least initially, requires more effort on the part of students and is not as comfortable for them. You may see your teaching ratings fall. However, the key is student motivation and a careful application of the motivational suggestions in Chapter Three should mitigate these negative effects. Also, teaching ratings generally improve over time.

Frecka offers the following suggestions to accounting faculty who want to introduce learning to learn into their courses.

1. Nothing is possible without motivated students. I would start with the strategies summary in Chapter Three and do my best to implement those suggestions.
2. Start small and experiment. In a very careful and detailed fashion, design, implement and assess a learning to learn module for one of your courses.
3. Read this monograph.
4. Identify a few "lightbulbs" that should turn on in students' minds throughout your course. For example, give students a bunch of cash transactions to keep track of in their checkbooks. After that, ask them to explain what they did with the cash. The question is very difficult to answer in a cash-based system. The lightbulb that should come on is that the double entry system and financial statements provide a very useful mechanism for answering questions like this.

Frecka offers these examples that can help students practice attributes of intentional learning:

1. Example of passive and active learning approach:
   Passive (fill in the blank): Accounting is often called the <u>language</u> of business.

Active: Why is accounting called the language of business? Ans. Because accounting provides useful information for economic decision-making.

Harder: What are the attributes of accounting information that make it useful?

2. Example of organizing:

There are three processes by which expenses get into the income statement (matching, systematic allocation, and period changes).

Explain what is meant by matching, systematic allocation and period costs. Give an example of a particular type of expense in explaining each of these concepts.

3. Example of connecting:

Deferred Revenue is to Revenue as <u>Assets</u> are to Expenses.

4. Example of organizing/connecting:

Prepare an entity diagram, for the entity Sandy Wilson, Rock Concert promoter.

5. Example of reflecting:

Why do you suppose that only some of the "assets" of the firm are reported on the firm's balance sheet?

Hints: (lower level support questions)

What's the accounting definition of an asset?

What are two requirements for reporting assets on the balance sheet?

## The University of Utah

James K. Loebbecke, Professor of Accounting and Associate Dean, reports that Utah modified the curriculum for the entire business program, both undergraduate and graduate, rather than just the accounting program. This provided a much greater commitment by administrators and acceptance by students than if it had been done for accounting alone. Loebbecke suggests the following as important in Utah's change process:

1. Involve the most influential members of the faculty in the questions of philosophy and design.

2. Communicate and get agreement from the entire faculty as you proceed.

3. Create a major, ongoing faculty development program that is implemented concurrently with curriculum changes.

4. Compensate faculty for course development through contracts and summer teaching innovation grants.

5. Phase the new curriculum in over a reasonable period of time.

## Arizona State University

ASU uses a cooperative learning activity which recognizes the importance of preparing students to be effective group learners. Professor Pat McKenzie provided this example:

BASIC ELEMENTS OF COOPERATIVE LEARNING GROUP ACTIVITY

PURPOSE: To learn about certain basic elements of cooperative learning by becoming "experts" and teaching your teammates.

DIRECTIONS: Look at your card and see if you hold a red (hearts or diamonds) or black (spades or clubs) suit.

If you are a Heart or Diamond you are to do the following:

1. In "Basic Elements of Cooperative Learning" read Positive Interdependence and Face to Face Promotive Interaction.

2. Also read "Cooperative Learning: Why Does It Work?"
3. The Heart and Diamond on the team should pair up and discuss how to teach the key points from the reading materials.
4. When you are comfortable with your teaching strategy, pair up with the Spade and Club duo and teach them.
5. When you are done, trade roles and let the Spade and Club teach you.

If you are a Spade or Club you are to do the following:

1. In "Basic Elements of Cooperative Learning" read Individual Accountability, Interpersonal and Small Group Skill and Group Processing.
2. Also read "What We Know About Cooperative Learning at the College Level."
3. The Spade and Club on the team should pair up and discuss how to teach the key points from the reading materials.
4. When you are comfortable with your teaching strategy, pair up with the Heart and Diamond duo and let them teach you.
5. When you are done, trade roles and you and your partner teach the Heart and Diamond duo.

REQUIRED: Within your group of four, make sure each member is clear on three aspects of Cooperative Learning: WHAT it is (facts, definitions); HOW it is used (procedures); and WHY it is effective (rationale, explanations).

## Brigham Young University

The BYU Integrated Junior Year Accounting Core was described in Chapter Four. This AECC grant project involved changing course content, method, administration, and sequencing. In a final report to the AECC, BYU faculty offered ten recommendations to those who may want to experiment with some of the changes that worked at Brigham Young.

1. Teach accounting courses from a systems perspective.
2. Integrate functional subject matter.
3. Introduce projects that develop written and oral communication skills in all courses.
4. Utilize group learning more widely.
5. Use written teaching plans in all courses to clearly establish course objectives.
6. Expand the grading system to include valid assessments of non-technical competencies.
7. Use examinations that test students' ability to think and reason rather than simply the ability to regurgitate memorized textbook material.
8. Integrate business law, ethics, international concepts, and current event topics in all courses.
9. Invite students to give honest and useful feedback on courses and teaching methodology and use that feedback to improve the course.
10. Initiate a faculty improvement program and reward faculty for innovative teaching.

As part of this change effort, BYU accounting faculty developed a number of new assignments for students: ethics cases, written and oral communication tasks, examination questions, and integrated business problem cases. Some of these are included in the report to the AECC. Interested faculty may want to contact BYU for examples.